MW00612672

Helping You Bring the Joy of the Faith to Your Family

Spiritual Journal

_____

my name

_____

_____

start date   end date

How to Use the Holy Heroes Spiritual Journal

There is no "wrong" way to use this journal: use it in *any way that helps you* listen more closely to God's Will for you each day.

You might want to use it in the morning to prepare for the day in prayer…or in the evening to review and remember God's blessings throughout the day…or to pause during the day to talk to God and your other friends in Heaven.

1. You'll find prayers for different *times of the day* in this journal—use them to raise your heart and mind to God.

2. The Prayer Prompt cards can help you. *Don't answer all the questions;* just select the ones that most appeal to you each day.

Choose one of the 4 Prayer Prompt cards provided with the Holy Heroes Spiritual Journal. Use the Prompt Card as both a bookmark (to keep your place as you write in the journal) and as an aid to your daily prayers and journalling.

There are prompts for your morning prayers on one side of the card and prompts for your nighttime prayers on the other side. Three of the Prompt Cards are designed to help you pray through the Church's liturgical seasons.

3. The Church has different "seasons" and "feast days" to help us focus on different aspects of the mystery of God's love for us. The Prayer Prompt cards and other information in this journal will help you unite your daily prayers to the Church's seasonal cycles.

4. *Write down your prayer lists and prayer intentions* to remind you to pray for others…and to see how God responds to your requests with His loving care!

5. Prepare for Confession and take our *Tear-Out Sheet for Confession* into the confessional with you.

What ideas do you have? We'd love to hear them! *Email us at Guides@HolyHeroes.com*

Some Saints' Feast Days

Below is a list of some of the *Holy Heroes Adventure Guides'* favorite saints and liturgical feasts.
Note: The Church moves the celebration of some of these feast days each year to accommodate Sundays, Lent, and Advent!

January
1: Mary, the Holy Mother of God
4: Saint Elizabeth Ann Seton
22: Day of Prayer for the Legal Protection of Unborn Children

February
2: The Presentation of the Lord
3: Saint Blaise
10: Saint José Sánchez del Río
20: Saints Francisco and Jacinta Marto
22: The Chair of Saint Peter the Apostle

March
3: Saint Katharine Drexel
17: Saint Patrick
19: Saint Joseph, Spouse of the Blessed Virgin Mary
25: The Annunciation of the Lord

April
16: Saint Bernadette Soubirous

May
1: Saint Joseph the Worker
13: Our Lady of Fatima and Blessed Imelda Lambertini
21: Saint Christopher Magallanes and Saint Miguel de la Mora
30: Saint Joan of Arc
31: The Visitation of the Blessed Virgin Mary

June
13: Saint Anthony of Padua
24: The Nativity of Saint John the Baptist
29: Saints Peter and Paul, Apostles

July
4: Blessed Pier Giorgio Frassati
6: Saint Maria Goretti
14: Saint Kateri Tekakwitha
16: Our Lady of Mount Carmel
26: Saints Joachim and Anne

August
6: The Transfiguration
11: Saint Clare
14: Saint Maximilian Kolbe
15: The Assumption of the Blessed Virgin Mary
23: Saint Rose of Lima
27: Saint Monica
28: Saint Augustine

September
5: Saint (Mother) Teresa of Calcutta
14: Exaltation of the Cross
15: Our Lady of Sorrows
29: Saints Michael, Gabriel, and Raphael, Archangels

October
1: Saint Therese of Lisieux
2: The Holy Guardian Angels
5: Saint Faustina Kowalska
22: Saint John Paul II

November
1: All Saints
2: All Souls
3: Saint Martin de Porres
22: Saint Cecilia
20: Blessed Miguel Pro

December
6: Saint Nicholas
8: The Immaculate Conception of the Blessed Virgin Mary
9: Saint Juan Diego
12: Our Lady of Guadalupe
13: Saint Lucy
25: Christmas
28: The Holy Innocents

*Get the exciting **Glory Stories Audio CDs**
featuring many of the saints listed above at*
www.HolyHeroes.com.

Prayers for Morning

Morning Offering

Oh, my Jesus, through the Immaculate Heart of Mary,
I offer You my prayers, works, joys, and sufferings of this day.
In union with the Holy Sacrifice of the Mass throughout the
world, I offer them for all the intentions of Your Sacred Heart,
for the intentions of my family and friends, and for the
intentions of our Holy Father, the Pope. Amen.

Guardian Angel

Angel of God, my guardian dear,
God's love for me has sent you here.
Ever this day, be at my side,
to light and guard, to rule and guide.
Amen.

Prayer for Midday

The Angelus

Leader: The angel of the Lord declared unto Mary,
All: And she conceived of the Holy Spirit.
[Hail, Mary]

Leader: Behold the handmaid of the Lord,
All: May it be done unto me according to thy word.
[Hail, Mary]

Leader: And the Word was made flesh,
All: (genuflecting) And dwelt among us.
[Hail, Mary]

Leader: Pray for us, O holy mother of God,
All: That we may be made worthy of the promises
of Christ.

Leader: Let us pray:
All: Pour forth, we beseech Thee, O Lord, Thy grace
into our hearts; that we to whom the incarnation of
Christ, Thy Son, was made known by the message of
an angel, may, by His Passion and Cross, be brought
to the glory of His Resurrection, through the same
Christ Our Lord. Amen.

---

*For more daily prayers, get the booklet **"Best-Loved Catholic Prayers"** at HolyHeroes.com.*

Prayers for Nighttime

Think back each evening about sins you committed during the day and ask God to forgive you and strengthen you against sinning tomorrow. If you sinned against anyone in your family and if they are still awake, you could apologize to them and ask for their forgiveness.

Filling in this Spiritual Journal and using the process for the Daily Examen on the next page is a good way to review your day .

You can also ask the Holy Spirit to inspire you with good resolutions for tomorrow.

Act of Contrition (asking God to forgive your sins of the day)
O my God, I am heartily sorry for having offended Thee, and I detest all my sins because I fear the loss of Heaven and the pains of Hell; but, most of all, because I have offended Thee, my God, Who art all good and worthy of all my love. And I firmly resolve, with the help of Thy grace, to confess my sins, to do penance, and to amend my life. Amen.

Prayer before sleeping (from the Liturgy of the Hours)
Protect us, Lord, as we stay awake,
Watch over us as we sleep,
That awake we may keep watch with Christ,
And asleep rest in His peace. Amen.

Nighttime blessing
"May the Lord bless you and keep you through the night and grant you peace."

Before you go to sleep each night, see if your mother or father will give you a simple blessing by tracing the Sign of the Cross on your forehead and saying a simple prayer, such as the one above.

Remember: God gave you as a gift to your family, selecting your mother and father as a gift for you, too. You can help them get to Heaven, and they can help you so that you will all be together as a family forever.

Praise to the Holy Trinity
Glory be to the Father,
And to the Son,
And to the Holy Spirit.
As it was in the beginning, is now,
and ever shall be, world without end.
Amen.

You can also end each day by making the Sign of the Cross yourself (with Holy Water, if you have any in your home), and saying a short prayer like the Glory Be above.

The Most Holy Rosary

Mysteries of the Rosary Assigned to Each Day of the Week

SUNDAY and WEDNESDAY
The Five Glorious Mysteries

The Resurrection (see Matthew 28:1–10)
The Ascension (see Acts 1:6-11)
The Descent of the Holy Spirit (see Acts 2:1-13)
The Assumption (see Revelations 12:1-3, 13-18)
The Coronation (see Revelations 12:1-5)

MONDAY and SATURDAY
The Five Joyful Mysteries

The Annunciation (see Luke 1:26–38)
The Visitation (see Luke 1:39–56)
The Nativity (see Luke 2:1–20)
The Presentation (see Luke 2:22–38)
The Finding of the Child Jesus in the Temple (see Luke 2:41–52)

TUESDAY and FRIDAY
The Five Sorrowful Mysteries

The Agony in the Garden (see Luke 22:39–46)
The Scourging at the Pillar (see Mark 15:6–15)
The Crowning with Thorns (see John 19:1–8)
The Carrying of the Cross (see John 19:16–20)
The Crucifixion (see John 19:25–30)

THURSDAY
The Five Luminous Mysteries

The Baptism of Jesus in the Jordan (see Matthew 3:13–17)
The Wedding Feast of Cana (see John 2:1–11)
The Proclamation of the Kingdom (see Mark 1:15, 2:3–13)
The Transfiguration (see Matthew 17:1–8)
The First Eucharist (see Matthew 26:26–32)

The Daily Examen

The Daily Examen is a way to pray about the events of your day so you can see God's loving presence beside you all the time and discover His Will for your life. Saint Ignatius Loyola, the founder of the Jesuits, created this five-step process.

Step 1

Pray to the Holy Spirit to allow you to see yourself and your actions in the day as God sees them. You may use your own words, perhaps something such as:

"Come, Holy Spirit, into my heart and my mind that I may truly see myself as God sees me, and behold in the events of today Your inspirations to goodness and Your love for me. Amen."

Now it's time to talk to Jesus as a friend: He was a child on earth in a family, too, and He grew up into an adult, just like you are doing. Just ask Him: Jesus wants to help you understand everything that happens to you!

Step 2

Reflect on all the gifts God has given you today in your life: the people, places, and things you encountered. Stir up gratitude in your heart with the help of the Holy Spirit!

Step 3

Think about what God has said to you today, in what He has allowed to happen to you. What do you think God was trying to ask you to do so you will grow in holiness every day, learning to love Him above all things and to love your neighbors (including your family!) as you love yourself? What do you think God was trying to tell you today?

Step 4

Now be honest about how you reacted to the events of today. Does one thing that happened stand out in your mind? How did you act? Were you joyful and unselfish? Did you commit any sins? Did you fail to do something good that you could have done? Tell God you are sorry for those unkind or selfish things you did today.

Step 5

Look forward to doing better for God tomorrow! Ask Jesus to tell you what He wants you to do to make tomorrow even better for you and for your family and friends. As Saint Paul said: "Brethren . . . one thing I do, forgetting what lies behind and straining forward to what lies ahead, I press on toward the goal for the prize of the upward call of God in Christ Jesus" (Philippians 3:13-14).

My Prayer List

People whom I know and pray for ...

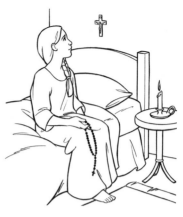

Praying for the living and the dead is a Spiritual Work of Mercy. List the people you want to pray for every day. If the person is dead, put a little cross next to his or her name.

My father: ————————————————————

My mother: ————————————————————

My grandparents: ———————————————————

My brothers and sisters: ——————————————————

——————————————————————————

My godparents: ———————————————————

Other people I know: ——————————————————

——————————————————————————

——————————————————————————

——————————————————————————

——————————————————————————

——————————————————————————

——————————————————————————

——————————————————————————

——————————————————————————

——————————————————————————

——————————————————————————

——————————————————————————

——————————————————————————

——————————————————————————

My Prayer List
More people whom I pray for ...

We are all related in the Body of Christ, so it is good to pray for people you don't even know. You will meet them in Heaven! List here other people to pray for, whether you have met them yet or not.

_____

_____

_____

_____

_____

_____

_____

_____

_____

_____

_____

_____

_____

_____

_____

_____

_____

_____

_____

My Prayer Intentions

Things I want to remember to pray for ...

List here things you need and want to pray for. You may also want to make a note next to your intentions about how God answers your prayers.

Lord, hear my prayer for:

God's answer:

More Prayer Intentions
Things that other people have asked me to pray for ...

List here things that other people have asked you to pray for.
You can also write how God answered those prayers.

Lord, hear my prayer for: God's answer:

About LENT

Lent is a season of penance and preparation, for when we renew our baptismal promises at Easter.

Lenten prayer, fasting, and almsgiving are intended to help create in our hearts an ever-larger capacity to love. By denying ourselves some things that are good and by sharing more with others, we die to ourselves a little—and grow more in love of God and neighbor.

Fasting

A fasting day means no more than one meal. If necessary, some food may be taken in the morning and evening *(which customarily should combine to be less than the full meal for the day)*.

Abstinence

Abstinence means to abstain, which is to deny something to oneself. In Lent we abstain from eating meat on certain days. Meat is defined as dishes principally or substantially comprised of the flesh of land-dwelling mammals and birds, but not sauces or gravies. Eggs and milk products are also allowed.

Lenten Rules for Fasting and Abstinence

Ash Wednesday:	Abstinence and Fasting
All Fridays:	Abstinence *(except Fridays celebrated as Solemnities)*
Good Friday:	Abstinence and Fasting

Who must abide by these rules

Abstinence: Everyone from age 14, unless a medical condition would be significantly affected by it

Fasting: Everyone aged 18 to 59 unless excused for a medical condition or other sufficient reason *(including pregnant or nursing women)*

Voluntary penances and spiritual practices

Most Catholics "give up" something pleasurable for Lent as a penance and take on additional spiritual practices, such as daily Mass or other prayers. Ask the Holy Spirit to inspire in you, during Lent, those practices that can help you grow in holiness!

Join us for Lenten Adventure!

It's a time-saver for Mom, great for the kids, and FREE family fun!

Virginia   Clara

Here's what you get for FREE:

Daily Lenten Activities
You'll receive regular emails linking you
to daily activities

Margaret   Trey

Fun video & audio selections
View and listen online to an array of
Holy Heroes media

Anna   Therese

Activity Downloads
Print out & enjoy coloring pages,
word searches, crossword puzzles, and more

Lillian   Caroline

Fun quizzes and much more!

Lenten Adventure **is brought to you by the**
Holy Heroes Adventure Guides!

(and the *Holy Heroes Answer Kid*, too!)

Register now at LentenAdventure.com!

(it's FREE, but you need to register)

About ADVENT

Advent is the Catholic Church's season of *preparation* for the celebration of Christmas.

During Advent, as we *prepare for Christmas*, it must be noted that many people in the culture around us are *already celebrating Christmas*—without having taken any time to prepare their hearts to welcome the Savior! We should embrace the Advent season as a true time of *preparation*.

How long is Advent?

Advent begins four Sundays before Christmas and continues until the evening of Christmas Eve. The first Sunday can be as early as November 27 or as late as December 3, so Advent can be as long as 28 days or as short as 22 days.

The First Sunday in Advent is the first day of the new Liturgical Year. During Advent we prepare ourselves for the coming of Christ in three ways:

1) Advent is a season to prepare for Christmas when **Christ's First Coming** to us is remembered.

2) Advent is a time to prepare our souls for the **coming of Christ to us individually** in every Holy Communion and in judgment at our death.

3) Advent is also a season when that remembrance directs the mind and heart to await **Christ's Second Coming** at the end of time.

Therefore, Advent is a period for devout and joyful expectation.

Join us for Advent Adventure!

Let our family take yours on the fun and easy *"Advent Adventure"*!

It's FREE—it costs you nothing, nada, zilch.

It's EASY—we do all the work for you, then we send you daily emails full of fun for ages 3 and up. You just click to watch short videos ... click to print off fun activities ... click to pray along with us!

Learn from the Holy Heroes *"Adventure Guides"* & the *"Answer Kid,"* too!

Trey   Margaret   Clara   Virginia

Caroline   Lillian   Therese   Anna

We do all the work for you, sending you daily emails full of fun:

- Prepare your heart for Jesus through our **Sacrifice Manger** activity!
- Make family memories as you explore **Advent Traditions** and **Feast Days** together!
- Get more out of the Mass with **"Mass prep" activities** for each Sunday of Advent!
- Learn the "big picture" of Salvation History through our **daily "Jesse Tree" activities!**
- **Fall in love with the Rosary.** Pray a "decade a day" and get "Rosary Certified" this Advent!
- And more ... with new stuff every year!

Register now at AdventAdventure.com!

(it's FREE, but you need to register)

Use the Prayer Prompts to help you pray quietly. Then journal on the lines below.

"Your words were found, and I ate them, and your words became to me a joy and the delight of my heart . . ."   Jeremiah 15:16
   (from the Short Reading for Week II, Lauds for Monday)

Jeremiah speaks of meditation on the Word of God, and its fruit.
   "I ate them" - chewed, swallowed, digested. Took them fully into myself, made them part of me. Partook of them fully.
   God's words "a joy" and "the delight of my heart" - here is the fruit of "eating" God's words.

I went to Mass today.   Yes   No

I prayed _____ decades of the Holy Rosary today.

I examined my conscience today.   Yes   No

I went to Confession today.   Yes   No

Days since my last Confession: _____ days.

I prayed my evening prayers tonight.   Yes   No

Day _____   Date _____

Feast or Holiday _____

I prayed my
morning prayers today.

Yes   *No*

Use the Prayer Prompts to help you pray quietly. Then journal on the lines below.

_____
_____
_____
_____
_____
_____
_____
_____
_____
_____
_____
_____
_____
_____

I went to Mass today.   *Yes*   *No*

I prayed _____ decades of the Holy Rosary today.

I examined my conscience today.   *Yes*   *No*

I went to Confession today.   *Yes*   *No*

Days since my last Confession: _____ days.

I prayed my evening prayers tonight.   *Yes*   *No*

Day _____ Date _____

Feast or Holiday _____

I prayed my
morning prayers today.

Yes   *No*

Use the Prayer Prompts to help you pray quietly. Then journal on the lines below.

....

....

....

....

....

....

....

....

....

....

....

....

....

....

....

....

I went to Mass today.   *Yes   No*

I prayed _____ decades of the Holy Rosary today.

I examined my conscience today.   *Yes   No*

I went to Confession today.   *Yes   No*

Days since my last Confession: _____ days.

I prayed my evening prayers tonight.   *Yes   No*

Day _____ Date _____

Feast or Holiday _____

I prayed my
morning prayers today.

Yes   *No*

Use the Prayer Prompts to help you pray quietly. Then journal on the lines below.

....

....

....

....

....

....

....

....

....

....

....

....

....

....

I went to Mass today.   *Yes*   *No*

I prayed _____ decades of the Holy Rosary today.

I examined my conscience today.   *Yes*   *No*

I went to Confession today.   *Yes*   *No*

Days since my last Confession: _____ days.

I prayed my evening prayers tonight.   *Yes*   *No*

Day _____ Date _____

Feast or Holiday _____

**I prayed my
morning prayers today.**

Yes   No

Use the Prayer Prompts to help you pray quietly. Then journal on the lines below.

_____

_____

_____

_____

_____

_____

_____

_____

_____

_____

_____

_____

_____

_____

_____

_____

I went to Mass today.   *Yes   No*

I prayed _____ decades of the Holy Rosary today.

I examined my conscience today.   *Yes   No*

I went to Confession today.   *Yes   No*

Days since my last Confession: _____ days.

I prayed my evening prayers tonight.   *Yes   No*

Day _____ Date _____

Feast or Holiday _____

I prayed my
morning prayers today.

Yes   *No*

Use the Prayer Prompts to help you pray quietly. Then journal on the lines below.

....

....

....

....

....

....

....

....

....

....

....

....

....

....

I went to Mass today.   *Yes   No*

I prayed _____ decades of the Holy Rosary today.

I examined my conscience today.   *Yes   No*

I went to Confession today.   *Yes   No*

Days since my last Confession: _____ days.

I prayed my evening prayers tonight.   *Yes   No*

Day _____ Date _____

Feast or Holiday _____

I prayed my morning prayers today.

Yes   No

Use the Prayer Prompts to help you pray quietly. Then journal on the lines below.

_____

_____

_____

_____

_____

_____

_____

_____

_____

_____

_____

_____

_____

_____

_____

I went to Mass today.   *Yes   No*

I prayed _____ decades of the Holy Rosary today.

I examined my conscience today.   *Yes   No*

I went to Confession today.   *Yes   No*

Days since my last Confession: _____ days.

I prayed my evening prayers tonight.   *Yes   No*

Day _____ Date _____

I prayed my
morning prayers today.

Feast or Holiday _____

Yes   *No*

Use the Prayer Prompts to help you pray quietly. Then journal on the lines below.

_____

_____

_____

_____

_____

_____

_____

_____

_____

_____

_____

_____

_____

_____

_____

_____

_____

I went to Mass today.   *Yes*   *No*

I prayed _____ decades of the Holy Rosary today.

I examined my conscience today.   *Yes*   *No*

I went to Confession today.   *Yes*   *No*

Days since my last Confession: _____ days.

I prayed my evening prayers tonight.   *Yes*   *No*

Day _____   Date _____

Feast or Holiday _____

I prayed my
morning prayers today.

Yes   *No*

Use the Prayer Prompts to help you pray quietly. Then journal on the lines below.

_____

_____

_____

_____

_____

_____

_____

_____

_____

_____

_____

_____

_____

_____

_____

_____

_____

_____

I went to Mass today.   *Yes*   *No*

I prayed _____ decades of the Holy Rosary today.

I examined my conscience today.   *Yes*   *No*

I went to Confession today.   *Yes*   *No*

Days since my last Confession: _____ days.

I prayed my evening prayers tonight.   *Yes*   *No*

Day _____ Date _____

Feast or Holiday _____

I prayed my
morning prayers today.

Yes   *No*

Use the Prayer Prompts to help you pray quietly. Then journal on the lines below.

....

....

....

....

....

....

....

....

....

....

....

....

....

....

....

....

....

I went to Mass today.   *Yes*   *No*

I prayed _____ decades of the Holy Rosary today.

I examined my conscience today.   *Yes*   *No*

I went to Confession today.   *Yes*   *No*

Days since my last Confession: _____ days.

I prayed my evening prayers tonight.   *Yes*   *No*

Day _____ Date _____

I prayed my
morning prayers today.

Feast or Holiday _____

Yes   No

Use the Prayer Prompts to help you pray quietly. Then journal on the lines below.

....

....

....

....

....

....

....

....

....

....

....

....

....

....

....

I went to Mass today.   *Yes   No*

I prayed _____ decades of the Holy Rosary today.

I examined my conscience today.   *Yes   No*

I went to Confession today.   *Yes   No*

Days since my last Confession: _____ days.

I prayed my evening prayers tonight.   *Yes   No*

Day _____ Date _____

Feast or Holiday _____

I prayed my
morning prayers today.

Yes   No

Use the Prayer Prompts to help you pray quietly. Then journal on the lines below.

....

....

....

....

....

....

....

....

....

....

....

....

....

....

....

I went to Mass today.   *Yes   No*

I prayed _____ decades of the Holy Rosary today.

I examined my conscience today.   *Yes   No*

I went to Confession today.   *Yes   No*

Days since my last Confession: _____ days.

I prayed my evening prayers tonight.   *Yes   No*

Day _____ Date _____

Feast or Holiday _____

I prayed my
morning prayers today.

Yes   *No*

Use the Prayer Prompts to help you pray quietly. Then journal on the lines below.

_____

_____

_____

_____

_____

_____

_____

_____

_____

_____

_____

_____

_____

_____

_____

_____

_____

I went to Mass today.   *Yes*   *No*

I prayed _____ decades of the Holy Rosary today.

I examined my conscience today.   *Yes*   *No*

I went to Confession today.   *Yes*   *No*

Days since my last Confession: _____ days.

I prayed my evening prayers tonight.   *Yes*   *No*

Day _____ Date _____

Feast or Holiday _____

I prayed my
morning prayers today.

Yes   *No*

Use the Prayer Prompts to help you pray quietly. Then journal on the lines below.

....

....

....

....

....

....

....

....

....

....

....

....

....

....

....

I went to Mass today.   *Yes*   *No*

I prayed _____ decades of the Holy Rosary today.

I examined my conscience today.   *Yes*   *No*

I went to Confession today.   *Yes*   *No*

Days since my last Confession: _____ days.

I prayed my evening prayers tonight.   *Yes*   *No*

Day _____ Date _____

Feast or Holiday _____

Use the Prayer Prompts to help you pray quietly. Then journal on the lines below.

_____

_____

_____

_____

_____

_____

_____

_____

_____

_____

_____

_____

_____

I went to Mass today.   *Yes   No*   I went to Confession today.   *Yes   No*

I prayed _____ decades of the Holy Rosary today.   Days since my last Confession: _____ days.

I examined my conscience today.   *Yes   No*   I prayed my evening prayers tonight.   *Yes   No*

Day _____   Date _____

Feast or Holiday _____

Use the Prayer Prompts to help you pray quietly. Then journal on the lines below.

_____

_____

_____

_____

_____

_____

_____

_____

_____

_____

_____

_____

_____

_____

_____

_____

I went to Mass today.   *Yes   No*

I prayed _____ decades of the Holy Rosary today.

I examined my conscience today.   *Yes   No*

I went to Confession today.   *Yes   No*

Days since my last Confession: _____ days.

I prayed my evening prayers tonight.   *Yes   No*

Day _____ Date _____

Feast or Holiday _____

I prayed my morning prayers today.

Yes   *No*

Use the Prayer Prompts to help you pray quietly. Then journal on the lines below.

....

....

....

....

....

....

....

....

....

....

....

....

....

....

....

I went to Mass today.   *Yes*   *No*

I prayed _____ decades of the Holy Rosary today.

I examined my conscience today.   *Yes*   *No*

I went to Confession today.   *Yes*   *No*

Days since my last Confession: _____ days.

I prayed my evening prayers tonight.   *Yes*   *No*

Day _____ Date _____

Feast or Holiday _____

I prayed my
morning prayers today.

Yes   *No*

Use the Prayer Prompts to help you pray quietly. Then journal on the lines below.

I went to Mass today.   *Yes*   *No*

I prayed _____ decades of the Holy Rosary today.

I examined my conscience today.   *Yes*   *No*

I went to Confession today.   *Yes*   *No*

Days since my last Confession: _____ days.

I prayed my evening prayers tonight.   *Yes*   *No*

Day _____ Date _____

Feast or Holiday _____

I prayed my
morning prayers today.

Yes   *No*

Use the Prayer Prompts to help you pray quietly. Then journal on the lines below.

....

....

....

....

....

....

....

....

....

....

....

....

....

....

....

....

....

....

I went to Mass today.   *Yes*   *No*

I prayed _____ decades of the Holy Rosary today.

I examined my conscience today.   *Yes*   *No*

I went to Confession today.   *Yes*   *No*

Days since my last Confession: _____ days.

I prayed my evening prayers tonight.   *Yes*   *No*

Day _____ Date _____

Feast or Holiday _____

I prayed my
morning prayers today.

Yes   No

Use the Prayer Prompts to help you pray quietly. Then journal on the lines below.

_____

_____

_____

_____

_____

_____

_____

_____

_____

_____

_____

_____

_____

_____

_____

_____

I went to Mass today.   Yes   No

I prayed _____ decades of the Holy Rosary today.

I examined my conscience today.   Yes   No

I went to Confession today.   Yes   No

Days since my last Confession: _____ days.

I prayed my evening prayers tonight.   Yes   No

Day _____   Date _____

Feast or Holiday _____

I prayed my
morning prayers today.

Yes   No

Use the Prayer Prompts to help you pray quietly. Then journal on the lines below.

....

....

....

....

....

....

....

....

....

....

....

....

....

....

I went to Mass today.   *Yes   No*

I prayed _____ decades of the Holy Rosary today.

I examined my conscience today.   *Yes   No*

I went to Confession today.   *Yes   No*

Days since my last Confession: _____ days.

I prayed my evening prayers tonight.   *Yes   No*

Day _____ Date _____

I prayed my
morning prayers today.

Feast or Holiday _____

Yes   *No*

Use the Prayer Prompts to help you pray quietly. Then journal on the lines below.

_____

_____

_____

_____

_____

_____

_____

_____

_____

_____

_____

_____

_____

_____

_____

_____

I went to Mass today.   *Yes*   *No*

I prayed _____ decades of the Holy Rosary today.

I examined my conscience today.   *Yes*   *No*

I went to Confession today.   *Yes*   *No*

Days since my last Confession: _____ days.

I prayed my evening prayers tonight.   *Yes*   *No*

Day _____ Date _____

Feast or Holiday _____

**I prayed my
morning prayers today.**

Yes   No

Use the Prayer Prompts to help you pray quietly. Then journal on the lines below.

....

....

....

....

....

....

....

....

....

....

....

....

....

I went to Mass today.   *Yes   No*

I prayed _____ decades of the Holy Rosary today.

I examined my conscience today.   *Yes   No*

I went to Confession today.   *Yes   No*

Days since my last Confession: _____ days.

I prayed my evening prayers tonight.   *Yes   No*

Day _____ Date _____

Feast or Holiday _____

I prayed my
morning prayers today.

Yes   *No*

Use the Prayer Prompts to help you pray quietly. Then journal on the lines below.

....

....

....

....

....

....

....

....

....

....

....

....

....

....

....

....

....

....

I went to Mass today.   *Yes*   *No*

I prayed _____ decades of the Holy Rosary today.

I examined my conscience today.   *Yes*   *No*

I went to Confession today.   *Yes*   *No*

Days since my last Confession: _____ days.

I prayed my evening prayers tonight.   *Yes*   *No*

Day _____   Date _____

Feast or Holiday _____

I prayed my
morning prayers today.

Yes   *No*

Use the Prayer Prompts to help you pray quietly. Then journal on the lines below.

I went to Mass today.   *Yes*   *No*

I prayed _____ decades of the Holy Rosary today.

I examined my conscience today.   *Yes*   *No*

I went to Confession today.   *Yes*   *No*

Days since my last Confession: _____ days.

I prayed my evening prayers tonight.   *Yes*   *No*

Day _____ Date _____

Feast or Holiday _____

**I prayed my
morning prayers today.**

Yes   No

Use the Prayer Prompts to help you pray quietly. Then journal on the lines below.

....

....

....

....

....

....

....

....

....

....

....

....

....

....

....

....

....

I went to Mass today.   *Yes   No*

I prayed _____ decades of the Holy Rosary today.

I examined my conscience today.   *Yes   No*

I went to Confession today.   *Yes   No*

Days since my last Confession: _____ days.

I prayed my evening prayers tonight.   *Yes   No*

Day _____ Date _____

Feast or Holiday _____

I prayed my
morning prayers today.

Yes   *No*

Use the Prayer Prompts to help you pray quietly. Then journal on the lines below.

....

....

....

....

....

....

....

....

....

....

....

....

....

....

....

....

I went to Mass today.   *Yes   No*

I prayed _____ decades of the Holy Rosary today.

I examined my conscience today.   *Yes   No*

I went to Confession today.   *Yes   No*

Days since my last Confession: _____ days.

I prayed my evening prayers tonight.   *Yes   No*

Day   Date _____

Feast or Holiday _____

I prayed my
morning prayers today.

Yes   No

Use the Prayer Prompts to help you pray quietly. Then journal on the lines below.

I went to Mass today.   *Yes   No*

I prayed _____ decades of the Holy Rosary today.

I examined my conscience today.   *Yes   No*

I went to Confession today.   *Yes   No*

Days since my last Confession: _____ days.

I prayed my evening prayers tonight.   *Yes   No*

Day _____ Date _____

Feast or Holiday _____

I prayed my
morning prayers today.

Yes   *No*

Use the Prayer Prompts to help you pray quietly. Then journal on the lines below.

....

....

....

....

....

....

....

....

....

....

....

....

....

....

....

....

....

....

....

....

I went to Mass today.   *Yes*   *No*

I prayed _____ decades of the Holy Rosary today.

I examined my conscience today.   *Yes*   *No*

I went to Confession today.   *Yes*   *No*

Days since my last Confession: _____ days.

I prayed my evening prayers tonight.   *Yes*   *No*

Use the Prayer Prompts to help you pray quietly. Then journal on the lines below.

....

....

....

....

....

....

....

....

....

....

....

....

....

....

....

....

....

....

I went to Mass today.   Yes   No

I prayed _____ decades of the Holy Rosary today.

I examined my conscience today.   Yes   No

I went to Confession today.   Yes   No

Days since my last Confession: _____ days.

I prayed my evening prayers tonight.   Yes   No

Day _____ Date _____

Feast or Holiday _____

**I prayed my
morning prayers today.**

Yes   *No*

Use the Prayer Prompts to help you pray quietly. Then journal on the lines below.

....

....

....

....

....

....

....

....

....

....

....

....

....

....

....

....

....

....

I went to Mass today.   *Yes*   *No*

I prayed _____ decades of the Holy Rosary today.

I examined my conscience today.   *Yes*   *No*

I went to Confession today.   *Yes*   *No*

Days since my last Confession: _____ days.

I prayed my evening prayers tonight.   *Yes*   *No*

Day _____ Date _____

Feast or Holiday _____

**I prayed my
morning prayers today.**

Yes   No

Use the Prayer Prompts to help you pray quietly. Then journal on the lines below.

_____

_____

_____

_____

_____

_____

_____

_____

_____

_____

_____

_____

_____

_____

_____

_____

I went to Mass today.   *Yes   No*

I prayed _____ decades of the Holy Rosary today.

I examined my conscience today.   *Yes   No*

I went to Confession today.   *Yes   No*

Days since my last Confession: _____ days.

I prayed my evening prayers tonight.   *Yes   No*

Day _____ Date _____

Feast or Holiday _____

**I prayed my
morning prayers today.**

Yes   No

Use the Prayer Prompts to help you pray quietly. Then journal on the lines below.

I went to Mass today.   *Yes   No*

I prayed _____ decades of the Holy Rosary today.

I examined my conscience today.   *Yes   No*

I went to Confession today.   *Yes   No*

Days since my last Confession: _____ days.

I prayed my evening prayers tonight.   *Yes   No*

Day _____ Date _____

Feast or Holiday _____

I prayed my
morning prayers today.

Yes   No

Use the Prayer Prompts to help you pray quietly. Then journal on the lines below.

....

....

....

....

....

....

....

....

....

....

....

....

....

....

I went to Mass today.   *Yes   No*

I prayed _____ decades of the Holy Rosary today.

I examined my conscience today.   *Yes   No*

I went to Confession today.   *Yes   No*

Days since my last Confession: _____ days.

I prayed my evening prayers tonight.   *Yes   No*

Day _____ Date _____

Feast or Holiday _____

**I prayed my
morning prayers today.**

Yes   No

Use the Prayer Prompts to help you pray quietly. Then journal on the lines below.

....

....

....

....

....

....

....

....

....

....

....

....

....

....

....

....

....

....

....

....

I went to Mass today.   *Yes   No*

I prayed _____ decades of the Holy Rosary today.

I examined my conscience today.   *Yes   No*

I went to Confession today.   *Yes   No*

Days since my last Confession: _____ days.

I prayed my evening prayers tonight.   *Yes   No*

Day _____ Date _____

Feast or Holiday _____

I prayed my
morning prayers today.

Yes   No

Use the Prayer Prompts to help you pray quietly. Then journal on the lines below.

....

....

....

....

....

....

....

....

....

....

....

....

....

....

....

....

....

....

....

I went to Mass today.   *Yes   No*

I prayed _____ decades of the Holy Rosary today.

I examined my conscience today.   *Yes   No*

I went to Confession today.   *Yes   No*

Days since my last Confession: _____ days.

I prayed my evening prayers tonight.   *Yes   No*

Day _____ Date _____

Feast or Holiday _____

I prayed my morning prayers today.

Yes   No

Use the Prayer Prompts to help you pray quietly. Then journal on the lines below.

....

....

....

....

....

....

....

....

....

....

....

....

....

....

....

....

....

....

....

....

I went to Mass today.   *Yes   No*

I prayed _____ decades of the Holy Rosary today.

I examined my conscience today.   *Yes   No*

I went to Confession today.   *Yes   No*

Days since my last Confession: _____ days.

I prayed my evening prayers tonight.   *Yes   No*

Day _____ Date _____

Feast or Holiday _____

**I prayed my
morning prayers today.**

Yes   No

Use the Prayer Prompts to help you pray quietly. Then journal on the lines below.

_____

_____

_____

_____

_____

_____

_____

_____

_____

_____

_____

_____

_____

_____

_____

_____

_____

_____

I went to Mass today.   *Yes   No*

I prayed _____ decades of the Holy Rosary today.

I examined my conscience today.   *Yes   No*

I went to Confession today.   *Yes   No*

Days since my last Confession: _____ days.

I prayed my evening prayers tonight.   *Yes   No*

Day _____ Date _____

I prayed my
morning prayers today.

Feast or Holiday _____

Yes   *No*

Use the Prayer Prompts to help you pray quietly. Then journal on the lines below.

....

....

....

....

....

....

....

....

....

....

....

....

....

....

I went to Mass today.   *Yes*   *No*

I prayed _____ decades of the Holy Rosary today.

I examined my conscience today.   *Yes*   *No*

I went to Confession today.   *Yes*   *No*

Days since my last Confession: _____ days.

I prayed my evening prayers tonight.   *Yes*   *No*

Day	Date	I prayed my morning prayers today.
Feast or Holiday		Yes No

Use the Prayer Prompts to help you pray quietly. Then journal on the lines below.

....

....

....

....

....

....

....

....

....

....

....

....

....

....

....

....

....

I went to Mass today.   Yes   No

I prayed _____ decades of the Holy Rosary today.

I examined my conscience today.   Yes   No

I went to Confession today.   Yes   No

Days since my last Confession: _____ days.

I prayed my evening prayers tonight.   Yes   No

Day _____ Date _____

Feast or Holiday _____

I prayed my morning prayers today.

Yes   *No*

Use the Prayer Prompts to help you pray quietly. Then journal on the lines below.

_____

_____

_____

_____

_____

_____

_____

_____

_____

_____

_____

_____

_____

_____

_____

_____

I went to Mass today.   *Yes*   *No*

I prayed _____ decades of the Holy Rosary today.

I examined my conscience today.   *Yes*   *No*

I went to Confession today.   *Yes*   *No*

Days since my last Confession: _____ days.

I prayed my evening prayers tonight.   *Yes*   *No*

Day _____ Date _____

Feast or Holiday _____

I prayed my
morning prayers today.

Yes   *No*

Use the Prayer Prompts to help you pray quietly. Then journal on the lines below.

I went to Mass today.   *Yes*   *No*

I prayed _____ decades of the Holy Rosary today.

I examined my conscience today.   *Yes*   *No*

I went to Confession today.   *Yes*   *No*

Days since my last Confession: _____ days.

I prayed my evening prayers tonight.   *Yes*   *No*

Day _____ Date _____

Feast or Holiday _____

**I prayed my
morning prayers today.**

Yes   No

Use the Prayer Prompts to help you pray quietly. Then journal on the lines below.

....

....

....

....

....

....

....

....

....

....

....

....

....

....

I went to Mass today.   *Yes   No*

I prayed _____ decades of the Holy Rosary today.

I examined my conscience today.   *Yes   No*

I went to Confession today.   *Yes   No*

Days since my last Confession: _____ days.

I prayed my evening prayers tonight.   *Yes   No*

Day _____ Date _____

Feast or Holiday _____

I prayed my
morning prayers today.

Yes   *No*

Use the Prayer Prompts to help you pray quietly. Then journal on the lines below.

_____

_____

_____

_____

_____

_____

_____

_____

_____

_____

_____

_____

_____

_____

_____

I went to Mass today.   *Yes*   *No*

I prayed _____ decades of the Holy Rosary today.

I examined my conscience today.   *Yes*   *No*

I went to Confession today.   *Yes*   *No*

Days since my last Confession: _____ days.

I prayed my evening prayers tonight.   *Yes*   *No*

Day _____   Date _____

Feast or Holiday _____

I prayed my
morning prayers today.

Yes   *No*

Use the Prayer Prompts to help you pray quietly. Then journal on the lines below.

....

....

....

....

....

....

....

....

....

....

....

....

....

....

....

....

....

....

I went to Mass today.   *Yes*   *No*

I prayed _____ decades of the Holy Rosary today.

I examined my conscience today.   *Yes*   *No*

I went to Confession today.   *Yes*   *No*

Days since my last Confession: _____ days.

I prayed my evening prayers tonight.   *Yes*   *No*

Day _____ Date _____

Feast or Holiday _____

I prayed my
morning prayers today.

Yes   *No*

Use the Prayer Prompts to help you pray quietly. Then journal on the lines below.

I went to Mass today.   *Yes*   *No*

I prayed _____ decades of the Holy Rosary today.

I examined my conscience today.   *Yes*   *No*

I went to Confession today.   *Yes*   *No*

Days since my last Confession: _____ days.

I prayed my evening prayers tonight.   *Yes*   *No*

Day _____ Date _____

Feast or Holiday _____

I prayed my morning prayers today.

Yes   *No*

Use the Prayer Prompts to help you pray quietly. Then journal on the lines below.

....

....

....

....

....

....

....

....

....

....

....

....

....

....

....

I went to Mass today.   *Yes*   *No*

I prayed _____ decades of the Holy Rosary today.

I examined my conscience today.   *Yes*   *No*

I went to Confession today.   *Yes*   *No*

Days since my last Confession: _____ days.

I prayed my evening prayers tonight.   *Yes*   *No*

Day _____ Date _____

Feast or Holiday _____

I prayed my
morning prayers today.

Yes   *No*

Use the Prayer Prompts to help you pray quietly. Then journal on the lines below.

I went to Mass today.   *Yes*   *No*

I prayed _____ decades of the Holy Rosary today.

I examined my conscience today.   *Yes*   *No*

I went to Confession today.   *Yes*   *No*

Days since my last Confession: _____ days.

I prayed my evening prayers tonight.   *Yes*   *No*

Day _____ Date _____

Feast or Holiday _____

I prayed my
morning prayers today.

Yes   *No*

Use the Prayer Prompts to help you pray quietly. Then journal on the lines below.

....

....

....

....

....

....

....

....

....

....

....

....

....

....

I went to Mass today.   *Yes*   *No*

I prayed _____ decades of the Holy Rosary today.

I examined my conscience today.   *Yes*   *No*

I went to Confession today.   *Yes*   *No*

Days since my last Confession: _____ days.

I prayed my evening prayers tonight.   *Yes*   *No*

Day _____ Date _____

Feast or Holiday _____

I prayed my morning prayers today.

Yes   No

Use the Prayer Prompts to help you pray quietly. Then journal on the lines below.

I went to Mass today.   *Yes   No*

I prayed _____ decades of the Holy Rosary today.

I examined my conscience today.   *Yes   No*

I went to Confession today.   *Yes   No*

Days since my last Confession: _____ days.

I prayed my evening prayers tonight.   *Yes   No*

Day _____ Date _____

Feast or Holiday _____

**I prayed my
morning prayers today.**

Yes   No

Use the Prayer Prompts to help you pray quietly. Then journal on the lines below.

....

....

....

....

....

....

....

....

....

....

....

....

....

I went to Mass today.   *Yes   No*

I prayed _____ decades of the Holy Rosary today.

I examined my conscience today.   *Yes   No*

I went to Confession today.   *Yes   No*

Days since my last Confession: _____ days.

I prayed my evening prayers tonight.   *Yes   No*

Day	Date	I prayed my
		morning prayers today.
Feast or Holiday		Yes No

Use the Prayer Prompts to help you pray quietly. Then journal on the lines below.

....

....

....

....

....

....

....

....

....

....

....

....

....

....

....

....

....

I went to Mass today.   Yes   No

I prayed _____ decades of the Holy Rosary today.

I examined my conscience today.   Yes   No

I went to Confession today.   Yes   No

Days since my last Confession: _____ days.

I prayed my evening prayers tonight.   Yes   No

Day _____ Date _____

Feast or Holiday _____

I prayed my
morning prayers today.

Yes   *No*

Use the Prayer Prompts to help you pray quietly. Then journal on the lines below.

_____

_____

_____

_____

_____

_____

_____

_____

_____

_____

_____

_____

_____

_____

_____

_____

I went to Mass today.   *Yes   No*

I prayed _____ decades of the Holy Rosary today.

I examined my conscience today.   *Yes   No*

I went to Confession today.   *Yes   No*

Days since my last Confession: _____ days.

I prayed my evening prayers tonight.   *Yes   No*

Day _____ Date _____

Feast or Holiday _____

I prayed my
morning prayers today.

Yes   No

Use the Prayer Prompts to help you pray quietly. Then journal on the lines below.

....

....

....

....

....

....

....

....

....

....

....

....

....

....

....

....

....

....

....

....

....

....

I went to Mass today.   *Yes   No*

I prayed _____ decades of the Holy Rosary today.

I examined my conscience today.   *Yes   No*

I went to Confession today.   *Yes   No*

Days since my last Confession: _____ days.

I prayed my evening prayers tonight.   *Yes   No*

Day _____ Date _____

Feast or Holiday _____

I prayed my
morning prayers today.

Yes   *No*

Use the Prayer Prompts to help you pray quietly. Then journal on the lines below.

_____

_____

_____

_____

_____

_____

_____

_____

_____

_____

_____

_____

_____

_____

_____

_____

_____

I went to Mass today.   *Yes*   *No*

I prayed _____ decades of the Holy Rosary today.

I examined my conscience today.   *Yes*   *No*

I went to Confession today.   *Yes*   *No*

Days since my last Confession: _____ days.

I prayed my evening prayers tonight.   *Yes*   *No*

Day _____ Date _____

Feast or Holiday _____

I prayed my
morning prayers today.

Yes   *No*

Use the Prayer Prompts to help you pray quietly. Then journal on the lines below.

....

....

....

....

....

....

....

....

....

....

....

....

....

....

....

I went to Mass today.   *Yes*   *No*

I prayed _____ decades of the Holy Rosary today.

I examined my conscience today.   *Yes*   *No*

I went to Confession today.   *Yes*   *No*

Days since my last Confession: _____ days.

I prayed my evening prayers tonight.   *Yes*   *No*

Day _____ Date _____

Feast or Holiday _____

I prayed my
morning prayers today.

Yes   *No*

Use the Prayer Prompts to help you pray quietly. Then journal on the lines below.

I went to Mass today.   *Yes*   *No*

I prayed _____ decades of the Holy Rosary today.

I examined my conscience today.   *Yes*   *No*

I went to Confession today.   *Yes*   *No*

Days since my last Confession: _____ days.

I prayed my evening prayers tonight.   *Yes*   *No*

Day _____ Date _____

Feast or Holiday _____

I prayed my
morning prayers today.

Yes   *No*

Use the Prayer Prompts to help you pray quietly. Then journal on the lines below.

....

....

....

....

....

....

....

....

....

....

....

....

....

....

....

....

I went to Mass today.   *Yes*   *No*

I prayed _____ decades of the Holy Rosary today.

I examined my conscience today.   *Yes*   *No*

I went to Confession today.   *Yes*   *No*

Days since my last Confession: _____ days.

I prayed my evening prayers tonight.   *Yes*   *No*

Day _____ Date _____

Feast or Holiday _____

I prayed my morning prayers today.

Yes   No

Use the Prayer Prompts to help you pray quietly. Then journal on the lines below.

_____
_____
_____
_____
_____
_____
_____
_____
_____
_____
_____
_____
_____
_____
_____

I went to Mass today.   *Yes   No*

I prayed _____ decades of the Holy Rosary today.

I examined my conscience today.   *Yes   No*

I went to Confession today.   *Yes   No*

Days since my last Confession: _____ days.

I prayed my evening prayers tonight.   *Yes   No*

Day _____ Date _____

Feast or Holiday _____

I prayed my morning prayers today.

Yes   *No*

Use the Prayer Prompts to help you pray quietly. Then journal on the lines below.

....

....

....

....

....

....

....

....

....

....

....

....

....

....

....

....

....

....

....

....

I went to Mass today.   *Yes*   *No*

I prayed _____ decades of the Holy Rosary today.

I examined my conscience today.   *Yes*   *No*

I went to Confession today.   *Yes*   *No*

Days since my last Confession: _____ days.

I prayed my evening prayers tonight.   *Yes*   *No*

Day _____ Date _____

Feast or Holiday _____

I prayed my morning prayers today.

Yes   No

Use the Prayer Prompts to help you pray quietly. Then journal on the lines below.

....

....

....

....

....

....

....

....

....

....

....

....

....

....

....

....

....

....

I went to Mass today.   *Yes   No*

I prayed _____ decades of the Holy Rosary today.

I examined my conscience today.   *Yes   No*

I went to Confession today.   *Yes   No*

Days since my last Confession: _____ days.

I prayed my evening prayers tonight.   *Yes   No*

Day _____ Date _____

Feast or Holiday _____

I prayed my
morning prayers today.

Yes   *No*

Use the Prayer Prompts to help you pray quietly. Then journal on the lines below.

I went to Mass today.   *Yes   No*
I prayed _____ decades of the Holy Rosary today.
I examined my conscience today.   *Yes   No*

I went to Confession today.   *Yes   No*
Days since my last Confession: _____ days.
I prayed my evening prayers tonight.   *Yes   No*

Day _____ Date _____

Feast or Holiday _____

I prayed my
morning prayers today.

Yes   No

Use the Prayer Prompts to help you pray quietly. Then journal on the lines below.

....

....

....

....

....

....

....

....

....

....

....

....

....

....

....

....

....

....

I went to Mass today.   *Yes   No*

I prayed _____ decades of the Holy Rosary today.

I examined my conscience today.   *Yes   No*

I went to Confession today.   *Yes   No*

Days since my last Confession: _____ days.

I prayed my evening prayers tonight.   *Yes   No*

Day _____   Date _____

Feast or Holiday _____

**I prayed my
morning prayers today.**

Yes   No

Use the Prayer Prompts to help you pray quietly. Then journal on the lines below.

_____

_____

_____

_____

_____

_____

_____

_____

_____

_____

_____

_____

_____

_____

I went to Mass today.   *Yes   No*

I prayed _____ decades of the Holy Rosary today.

I examined my conscience today.   *Yes   No*

I went to Confession today.   *Yes   No*

Days since my last Confession: _____ days.

I prayed my evening prayers tonight.   *Yes   No*

Day _____ Date _____

Feast or Holiday _____

I prayed my morning prayers today.

Yes   No

Use the Prayer Prompts to help you pray quietly. Then journal on the lines below.

_____

_____

_____

_____

_____

_____

_____

_____

_____

_____

_____

_____

_____

_____

I went to Mass today.   *Yes   No*

I prayed _____ decades of the Holy Rosary today.

I examined my conscience today.   *Yes   No*

I went to Confession today.   *Yes   No*

Days since my last Confession: _____ days.

I prayed my evening prayers tonight.   *Yes   No*

Day _____ Date _____

Feast or Holiday _____

I prayed my
morning prayers today.

Yes   *No*

Use the Prayer Prompts to help you pray quietly. Then journal on the lines below.

....

....

....

....

....

....

....

....

....

....

....

....

....

....

....

I went to Mass today.   *Yes*   *No*

I prayed _____ decades of the Holy Rosary today.

I examined my conscience today.   *Yes*   *No*

I went to Confession today.   *Yes*   *No*

Days since my last Confession: _____ days.

I prayed my evening prayers tonight.   *Yes*   *No*

Day _____ Date _____

Feast or Holiday _____

**I prayed my
morning prayers today.**

Yes   No

Use the Prayer Prompts to help you pray quietly. Then journal on the lines below.

_____

_____

_____

_____

_____

_____

_____

_____

_____

_____

_____

_____

_____

_____

_____

_____

_____

_____

_____

_____

_____

I went to Mass today.   *Yes   No*

I prayed _____ decades of the Holy Rosary today.

I examined my conscience today.   *Yes   No*

I went to Confession today.   *Yes   No*

Days since my last Confession: _____ days.

I prayed my evening prayers tonight.   *Yes   No*

Day _____ Date _____

Feast or Holiday _____

I prayed my morning prayers today.

Yes   *No*

Use the Prayer Prompts to help you pray quietly. Then journal on the lines below.

_____

_____

_____

_____

_____

_____

_____

_____

_____

_____

_____

_____

_____

_____

_____

_____

_____

I went to Mass today.   *Yes*   *No*

I prayed _____ decades of the Holy Rosary today.

I examined my conscience today.   *Yes*   *No*

I went to Confession today.   *Yes*   *No*

Days since my last Confession: _____ days.

I prayed my evening prayers tonight.   *Yes*   *No*

Day _____ Date _____

I prayed my
morning prayers today.

Feast or Holiday _____

Yes   No

Use the Prayer Prompts to help you pray quietly. Then journal on the lines below.

....

....

....

....

....

....

....

....

....

....

....

....

....

....

I went to Mass today.   *Yes   No*

I prayed _____ decades of the Holy Rosary today.

I examined my conscience today.   *Yes   No*

I went to Confession today.   *Yes   No*

Days since my last Confession: _____ days.

I prayed my evening prayers tonight.   *Yes   No*

Day _____ Date _____

Feast or Holiday _____

I prayed my
morning prayers today.

Yes   *No*

Use the Prayer Prompts to help you pray quietly. Then journal on the lines below.

....

....

....

....

....

....

....

....

....

....

....

....

....

....

....

....

....

....

....

I went to Mass today.   *Yes*   *No*

I prayed _____ decades of the Holy Rosary today.

I examined my conscience today.   *Yes*   *No*

I went to Confession today.   *Yes*   *No*

Days since my last Confession: _____ days.

I prayed my evening prayers tonight.   *Yes*   *No*

Day _____ Date _____

Feast or Holiday _____

**I prayed my
morning prayers today.**

Yes   *No*

Use the Prayer Prompts to help you pray quietly. Then journal on the lines below.

_____

_____

_____

_____

_____

_____

_____

_____

_____

_____

_____

_____

_____

_____

I went to Mass today.   *Yes*   *No*

I prayed _____ decades of the Holy Rosary today.

I examined my conscience today.   *Yes*   *No*

I went to Confession today.   *Yes*   *No*

Days since my last Confession: _____ days.

I prayed my evening prayers tonight.   *Yes*   *No*

Use the Prayer Prompts to help you pray quietly. Then journal on the lines below.

I went to Mass today.   *Yes*   *No*

I prayed _____ decades of the Holy Rosary today.

I examined my conscience today.   *Yes*   *No*

I went to Confession today.   *Yes*   *No*

Days since my last Confession: _____ days.

I prayed my evening prayers tonight.   *Yes*   *No*

Day _____ Date _____

Feast or Holiday _____

**I prayed my
morning prayers today.**

Yes   *No*

Use the Prayer Prompts to help you pray quietly. Then journal on the lines below.

....

....

....

....

....

....

....

....

....

....

....

....

....

....

I went to Mass today.   *Yes   No*

I prayed _____ decades of the Holy Rosary today.

I examined my conscience today.   *Yes   No*

I went to Confession today.   *Yes   No*

Days since my last Confession: _____ days.

I prayed my evening prayers tonight.   *Yes   No*

Day _____ Date _____

Feast or Holiday _____

I prayed my
morning prayers today.

Yes   *No*

Use the Prayer Prompts to help you pray quietly. Then journal on the lines below.

....

....

....

....

....

....

....

....

....

....

....

....

....

....

I went to Mass today.   *Yes*   *No*

I prayed _____ decades of the Holy Rosary today.

I examined my conscience today.   *Yes*   *No*

I went to Confession today.   *Yes*   *No*

Days since my last Confession: _____ days.

I prayed my evening prayers tonight.   *Yes*   *No*

Day _____ Date _____

Feast or Holiday _____

I prayed my
morning prayers today.

Yes   *No*

Use the Prayer Prompts to help you pray quietly. Then journal on the lines below.

I went to Mass today.   *Yes*   *No*

I prayed _____ decades of the Holy Rosary today.

I examined my conscience today.   *Yes*   *No*

I went to Confession today.   *Yes*   *No*

Days since my last Confession: _____ days.

I prayed my evening prayers tonight.   *Yes*   *No*

Day _____ Date _____

Feast or Holiday _____

**I prayed my
morning prayers today.**

Yes   No

Use the Prayer Prompts to help you pray quietly. Then journal on the lines below.

I went to Mass today.   *Yes   No*

I prayed _____ decades of the Holy Rosary today.

I examined my conscience today.   *Yes   No*

I went to Confession today.   *Yes   No*

Days since my last Confession: _____ days.

I prayed my evening prayers tonight.   *Yes   No*

Day _____ Date _____

Feast or Holiday _____

I prayed my
morning prayers today.

Yes   *No*

Use the Prayer Prompts to help you pray quietly. Then journal on the lines below.

....

....

....

....

....

....

....

....

....

....

....

....

....

....

....

....

I went to Mass today.   *Yes*   *No*

I prayed _____ decades of the Holy Rosary today.

I examined my conscience today.   *Yes*   *No*

I went to Confession today.   *Yes*   *No*

Days since my last Confession: _____ days.

I prayed my evening prayers tonight.   *Yes*   *No*

Day _____ Date _____

I prayed my
morning prayers today.

Feast or Holiday _____

Yes   No

Use the Prayer Prompts to help you pray quietly. Then journal on the lines below.

I went to Mass today.   *Yes   No*
I prayed _____ decades of the Holy Rosary today.
I examined my conscience today.   *Yes   No*

I went to Confession today.   *Yes   No*
Days since my last Confession: _____ days.
I prayed my evening prayers tonight.   *Yes   No*

Day _____ Date _____

Feast or Holiday _____

I prayed my morning prayers today.

Yes   *No*

Use the Prayer Prompts to help you pray quietly. Then journal on the lines below.

....

....

....

....

....

....

....

....

....

....

....

....

....

....

....

....

I went to Mass today.   *Yes*   *No*

I prayed _____ decades of the Holy Rosary today.

I examined my conscience today.   *Yes*   *No*

I went to Confession today.   *Yes*   *No*

Days since my last Confession: _____ days.

I prayed my evening prayers tonight.   *Yes*   *No*

Use the Prayer Prompts to help you pray quietly. Then journal on the lines below.

....

....

....

....

....

....

....

....

....

....

....

....

....

....

....

....

....

I went to Mass today.   *Yes   No*

I prayed _____ decades of the Holy Rosary today.

I examined my conscience today.   *Yes   No*

I went to Confession today.   *Yes   No*

Days since my last Confession: _____ days.

I prayed my evening prayers tonight.   *Yes   No*

Day _____ Date _____

Feast or Holiday _____

I prayed my morning prayers today.

Yes   No

Use the Prayer Prompts to help you pray quietly. Then journal on the lines below.

....

....

....

....

....

....

....

....

....

....

....

....

....

....

I went to Mass today.   *Yes   No*

I prayed _____ decades of the Holy Rosary today.

I examined my conscience today.   *Yes   No*

I went to Confession today.   *Yes   No*

Days since my last Confession: _____ days.

I prayed my evening prayers tonight.   *Yes   No*

Day _____ Date _____

Feast or Holiday _____

I prayed my
morning prayers today.

Yes   *No*

Use the Prayer Prompts to help you pray quietly. Then journal on the lines below.

....

....

....

....

....

....

....

....

....

....

....

....

....

....

....

....

....

I went to Mass today.   *Yes   No*

I prayed _____ decades of the Holy Rosary today.

I examined my conscience today.   *Yes   No*

I went to Confession today.   *Yes   No*

Days since my last Confession: _____ days.

I prayed my evening prayers tonight.   *Yes   No*

Use the Prayer Prompts to help you pray quietly. Then journal on the lines below.

....

....

....

....

....

....

....

....

....

....

....

....

....

....

....

....

....

....

I went to Mass today.   Yes   No

I prayed _____ decades of the Holy Rosary today.

I examined my conscience today.   Yes   No

I went to Confession today.   Yes   No

Days since my last Confession: _____ days.

I prayed my evening prayers tonight.   Yes   No

Use the Prayer Prompts to help you pray quietly. Then journal on the lines below.

....

....

....

....

....

....

....

....

....

....

....

....

....

....

I went to Mass today.   *Yes   No*

I prayed _____ decades of the Holy Rosary today.

I examined my conscience today.   *Yes   No*

I went to Confession today.   *Yes   No*

Days since my last Confession: _____ days.

I prayed my evening prayers tonight.   *Yes   No*

Day _____ Date _____

Feast or Holiday _____

I prayed my
morning prayers today.

Yes   *No*

Use the Prayer Prompts to help you pray quietly. Then journal on the lines below.

_____

_____

_____

_____

_____

_____

_____

_____

_____

_____

_____

_____

_____

_____

_____

_____

_____

_____

I went to Mass today.   *Yes*   *No*

I prayed _____ decades of the Holy Rosary today.

I examined my conscience today.   *Yes*   *No*

I went to Confession today.   *Yes*   *No*

Days since my last Confession: _____ days.

I prayed my evening prayers tonight.   *Yes*   *No*

Day _____ Date _____

Feast or Holiday _____

**I prayed my
morning prayers today.**

Yes   No

Use the Prayer Prompts to help you pray quietly. Then journal on the lines below.

_____

_____

_____

_____

_____

_____

_____

_____

_____

_____

_____

_____

_____

_____

_____

_____

I went to Mass today.   *Yes   No*

I prayed _____ decades of the Holy Rosary today.

I examined my conscience today.   *Yes   No*

I went to Confession today.   *Yes   No*

Days since my last Confession: _____ days.

I prayed my evening prayers tonight.   *Yes   No*

Day _____ Date _____

Feast or Holiday _____

I prayed my morning prayers today.

Yes   No

Use the Prayer Prompts to help you pray quietly. Then journal on the lines below.

_____

_____

_____

_____

_____

_____

_____

_____

_____

_____

_____

_____

_____

_____

_____

_____

_____

_____

I went to Mass today.   *Yes   No*

I prayed _____ decades of the Holy Rosary today.

I examined my conscience today.   *Yes   No*

I went to Confession today.   *Yes   No*

Days since my last Confession: _____ days.

I prayed my evening prayers tonight.   *Yes   No*

Day _____   Date _____

Feast or Holiday _____

I prayed my
morning prayers today.

Yes   *No*

Use the Prayer Prompts to help you pray quietly. Then journal on the lines below.

....

....

....

....

....

....

....

....

....

....

....

....

....

....

....

....

I went to Mass today.   *Yes*   *No*

I prayed _____ decades of the Holy Rosary today.

I examined my conscience today.   *Yes*   *No*

I went to Confession today.   *Yes*   *No*

Days since my last Confession: _____ days.

I prayed my evening prayers tonight.   *Yes*   *No*

Day _____ Date _____

Feast or Holiday _____

I prayed my morning prayers today.
Yes   No

Use the Prayer Prompts to help you pray quietly. Then journal on the lines below.

_____

_____

_____

_____

_____

_____

_____

_____

_____

_____

_____

_____

_____

_____

I went to Mass today.   *Yes   No*

I prayed _____ decades of the Holy Rosary today.

I examined my conscience today.   *Yes   No*

I went to Confession today.   *Yes   No*

Days since my last Confession: _____ days.

I prayed my evening prayers tonight.   *Yes   No*

Use the Prayer Prompts to help you pray quietly. Then journal on the lines below.

....

....

....

....

....

....

....

....

....

....

....

....

....

....

....

....

....

I went to Mass today.   *Yes*   *No*

I prayed _____ decades of the Holy Rosary today.

I examined my conscience today.   *Yes*   *No*

I went to Confession today.   *Yes*   *No*

Days since my last Confession: _____ days.

I prayed my evening prayers tonight.   *Yes*   *No*

Day _____ Date _____

Feast or Holiday _____

I prayed my
morning prayers today.

Yes   *No*

Use the Prayer Prompts to help you pray quietly. Then journal on the lines below.

....

....

....

....

....

....

....

....

....

....

....

....

....

I went to Mass today.   *Yes*   *No*

I prayed _____ decades of the Holy Rosary today.

I examined my conscience today.   *Yes*   *No*

I went to Confession today.   *Yes*   *No*

Days since my last Confession: _____ days.

I prayed my evening prayers tonight.   *Yes*   *No*

Day _____ Date _____

Feast or Holiday _____

Use the Prayer Prompts to help you pray quietly. Then journal on the lines below.

I went to Mass today.   *Yes*   *No*

I prayed _____ decades of the Holy Rosary today.

I examined my conscience today.   *Yes*   *No*

I went to Confession today.   *Yes*   *No*

Days since my last Confession: _____ days.

I prayed my evening prayers tonight.   *Yes*   *No*

Day _____ Date _____

Feast or Holiday _____

**I prayed my
morning prayers today.**

Yes   *No*

Use the Prayer Prompts to help you pray quietly. Then journal on the lines below.

I went to Mass today.   *Yes*   *No*

I prayed _____ decades of the Holy Rosary today.

I examined my conscience today.   *Yes*   *No*

I went to Confession today.   *Yes*   *No*

Days since my last Confession: _____ days.

I prayed my evening prayers tonight.   *Yes*   *No*

Use the Prayer Prompts to help you pray quietly. Then journal on the lines below.

....

....

....

....

....

....

....

....

....

....

....

....

....

....

I went to Mass today.   Yes   No

I prayed _____ decades of the Holy Rosary today.

I examined my conscience today.   Yes   No

I went to Confession today.   Yes   No

Days since my last Confession: _____ days.

I prayed my evening prayers tonight.   Yes   No

Day _____ Date _____

Feast or Holiday _____

I prayed my morning prayers today.

Yes   *No*

Use the Prayer Prompts to help you pray quietly. Then journal on the lines below.

I went to Mass today.   *Yes*   *No*

I prayed _____ decades of the Holy Rosary today.

I examined my conscience today.   *Yes*   *No*

I went to Confession today.   *Yes*   *No*

Days since my last Confession: _____ days.

I prayed my evening prayers tonight.   *Yes*   *No*

Day _____ Date _____

Feast or Holiday _____

**I prayed my
morning prayers today.**

Yes   No

Use the Prayer Prompts to help you pray quietly. Then journal on the lines below.

_____

_____

_____

_____

_____

_____

_____

_____

_____

_____

_____

_____

_____

_____

_____

I went to Mass today.   *Yes   No*

I prayed _____ decades of the Holy Rosary today.

I examined my conscience today.   *Yes   No*

I went to Confession today.   *Yes   No*

Days since my last Confession: _____ days.

I prayed my evening prayers tonight.   *Yes   No*

Day _____ Date _____

Feast or Holiday _____

**I prayed my
morning prayers today.**

Yes   No

Use the Prayer Prompts to help you pray quietly. Then journal on the lines below.

I went to Mass today.   *Yes   No*

I prayed _____ decades of the Holy Rosary today.

I examined my conscience today.   *Yes   No*

I went to Confession today.   *Yes   No*

Days since my last Confession: _____ days.

I prayed my evening prayers tonight.   *Yes   No*

Use the Prayer Prompts to help you pray quietly. Then journal on the lines below.

....

....

....

....

....

....

....

....

....

....

....

....

....

....

....

....

....

I went to Mass today.   *Yes*   *No*

I prayed _____ decades of the Holy Rosary today.

I examined my conscience today.   *Yes*   *No*

I went to Confession today.   *Yes*   *No*

Days since my last Confession: _____ days.

I prayed my evening prayers tonight.   *Yes*   *No*

Day _____ Date _____

Feast or Holiday _____

**I prayed my
morning prayers today.**

Yes   No

Use the Prayer Prompts to help you pray quietly. Then journal on the lines below.

_____

_____

_____

_____

_____

_____

_____

_____

_____

_____

_____

_____

_____

_____

_____

_____

I went to Mass today.   *Yes   No*

I prayed _____ decades of the Holy Rosary today.

I examined my conscience today.   *Yes   No*

I went to Confession today.   *Yes   No*

Days since my last Confession: _____ days.

I prayed my evening prayers tonight.   *Yes   No*

Use the Prayer Prompts to help you pray quietly. Then journal on the lines below.

....

....

....

....

....

....

....

....

....

....

....

....

....

....

....

....

....

....

I went to Mass today.   *Yes*   *No*

I prayed _____ decades of the Holy Rosary today.

I examined my conscience today.   *Yes*   *No*

I went to Confession today.   *Yes*   *No*

Days since my last Confession: _____ days.

I prayed my evening prayers tonight.   *Yes*   *No*

Day _____ Date _____

Feast or Holiday _____

I prayed my morning prayers today.

Yes   *No*

Use the Prayer Prompts to help you pray quietly. Then journal on the lines below.

_____
_____
_____
_____
_____
_____
_____
_____
_____
_____
_____
_____
_____
_____
_____
_____
_____

I went to Mass today.   *Yes   No*

I prayed _____ decades of the Holy Rosary today.

I examined my conscience today.   *Yes   No*

I went to Confession today.   *Yes   No*

Days since my last Confession: _____ days.

I prayed my evening prayers tonight.   *Yes   No*

Day _____ Date _____

Feast or Holiday _____

I prayed my morning prayers today.

Yes   No

Use the Prayer Prompts to help you pray quietly. Then journal on the lines below.

....

....

....

....

....

....

....

....

....

....

....

....

....

....

....

....

....

....

I went to Mass today.   *Yes   No*

I prayed _____ decades of the Holy Rosary today.

I examined my conscience today.   *Yes   No*

I went to Confession today.   *Yes   No*

Days since my last Confession: _____ days.

I prayed my evening prayers tonight.   *Yes   No*

Day _____ Date _____

Feast or Holiday _____

Use the Prayer Prompts to help you pray quietly. Then journal on the lines below.

....

....

....

....

....

....

....

....

....

....

....

....

....

....

....

....

I went to Mass today.　*Yes*　*No*

I prayed _____ decades of the Holy Rosary today.

I examined my conscience today.　*Yes*　*No*

I went to Confession today.　*Yes*　*No*

Days since my last Confession: _____ days.

I prayed my evening prayers tonight.　*Yes*　*No*

Day _____ Date _____

Feast or Holiday _____

Use the Prayer Prompts to help you pray quietly. Then journal on the lines below.

....

....

....

....

....

....

....

....

....

....

....

....

....

....

....

....

I went to Mass today.   *Yes   No*

I prayed _____ decades of the Holy Rosary today.

I examined my conscience today.   *Yes   No*

I went to Confession today.   *Yes   No*

Days since my last Confession: _____ days.

I prayed my evening prayers tonight.   *Yes   No*

Day _____ Date _____

Feast or Holiday _____

I prayed my
morning prayers today.

Yes   *No*

Use the Prayer Prompts to help you pray quietly. Then journal on the lines below.

....

....

....

....

....

....

....

....

....

....

....

....

....

....

....

I went to Mass today.   *Yes*   *No*

I prayed _____ decades of the Holy Rosary today.

I examined my conscience today.   *Yes*   *No*

I went to Confession today.   *Yes*   *No*

Days since my last Confession: _____ days.

I prayed my evening prayers tonight.   *Yes*   *No*

Day _____ Date _____

Feast or Holiday _____

Use the Prayer Prompts to help you pray quietly. Then journal on the lines below.

_____

_____

_____

_____

_____

_____

_____

_____

_____

_____

_____

_____

_____

_____

I went to Mass today.   Yes   No

I prayed _____ decades of the Holy Rosary today.

I examined my conscience today.   Yes   No

I went to Confession today.   Yes   No

Days since my last Confession: _____ days.

I prayed my evening prayers tonight.   Yes   No

Day _____ Date _____

Feast or Holiday _____

**I prayed my
morning prayers today.**

Yes   *No*

Use the Prayer Prompts to help you pray quietly. Then journal on the lines below.

....

....

....

....

....

....

....

....

....

....

....

....

....

....

....

....

I went to Mass today.   *Yes   No*

I prayed _____ decades of the Holy Rosary today.

I examined my conscience today.   *Yes   No*

I went to Confession today.   *Yes   No*

Days since my last Confession: _____ days.

I prayed my evening prayers tonight.   *Yes   No*

Day _____ Date _____

Feast or Holiday _____

Use the Prayer Prompts to help you pray quietly. Then journal on the lines below.

....

....

....

....

....

....

....

....

....

....

....

....

....

....

....

....

....

....

I went to Mass today.   *Yes*   *No*

I prayed _____ decades of the Holy Rosary today.

I examined my conscience today.   *Yes*   *No*

I went to Confession today.   *Yes*   *No*

Days since my last Confession: _____ days.

I prayed my evening prayers tonight.   *Yes*   *No*

Day _____ Date _____

Feast or Holiday _____

I prayed my
morning prayers today.

Yes   No

Use the Prayer Prompts to help you pray quietly. Then journal on the lines below.

....
....
....
....
....
....
....
....
....
....
....
....
....
....
....
....
....

I went to Mass today.   Yes   No

I prayed _____ decades of the Holy Rosary today.

I examined my conscience today.   Yes   No

I went to Confession today.   Yes   No

Days since my last Confession: _____ days.

I prayed my evening prayers tonight.   Yes   No

Day _____ Date _____

Feast or Holiday _____

I prayed my morning prayers today.

Yes   *No*

Use the Prayer Prompts to help you pray quietly. Then journal on the lines below.

....

....

....

....

....

....

....

....

....

....

....

....

....

....

I went to Mass today.   *Yes*   *No*

I prayed _____ decades of the Holy Rosary today.

I examined my conscience today.   *Yes*   *No*

I went to Confession today.   *Yes*   *No*

Days since my last Confession: _____ days.

I prayed my evening prayers tonight.   *Yes*   *No*

Day _____   Date _____

Feast or Holiday _____

I prayed my
morning prayers today.

Yes   No

Use the Prayer Prompts to help you pray quietly. Then journal on the lines below.

....

....

....

....

....

....

....

....

....

....

....

....

....

....

I went to Mass today.   *Yes   No*

I prayed _____ decades of the Holy Rosary today.

I examined my conscience today.   *Yes   No*

I went to Confession today.   *Yes   No*

Days since my last Confession: _____ days.

I prayed my evening prayers tonight.   *Yes   No*

Use the Prayer Prompts to help you pray quietly. Then journal on the lines below.

....

....

....

....

....

....

....

....

....

....

....

....

....

....

....

....

....

....

Day _____ Date _____

Feast or Holiday _____

Use the Prayer Prompts to help you pray quietly. Then journal on the lines below.

....

....

....

....

....

....

....

....

....

....

....

....

....

....

I went to Mass today.   Yes   No

I prayed _____ decades of the Holy Rosary today.

I examined my conscience today.   Yes   No

I went to Confession today.   Yes   No

Days since my last Confession: _____ days.

I prayed my evening prayers tonight.   Yes   No

Day _____ Date _____

Feast or Holiday _____

I prayed my
morning prayers today.

Yes   No

Use the Prayer Prompts to help you pray quietly. Then journal on the lines below.

....

....

....

....

....

....

....

....

....

....

....

....

....

....

....

....

....

....

....

I went to Mass today.   *Yes   No*

I prayed _____ decades of the Holy Rosary today.

I examined my conscience today.   *Yes   No*

I went to Confession today.   *Yes   No*

Days since my last Confession: _____ days.

I prayed my evening prayers tonight.   *Yes   No*

Day _____ Date _____

Feast or Holiday _____

**I prayed my
morning prayers today.**

Yes   No

Use the Prayer Prompts to help you pray quietly. Then journal on the lines below.

_____

_____

_____

_____

_____

_____

_____

_____

_____

_____

_____

_____

_____

_____

_____

_____

_____

I went to Mass today.   *Yes   No*

I prayed _____ decades of the Holy Rosary today.

I examined my conscience today.   *Yes   No*

I went to Confession today.   *Yes   No*

Days since my last Confession: _____ days.

I prayed my evening prayers tonight.   *Yes   No*

Day _____ Date _____

Feast or Holiday _____

**I prayed my
morning prayers today.**

Yes   No

Use the Prayer Prompts to help you pray quietly. Then journal on the lines below.

_____

_____

_____

_____

_____

_____

_____

_____

_____

_____

_____

_____

_____

I went to Mass today.   *Yes   No*

I prayed _____ decades of the Holy Rosary today.

I examined my conscience today.   *Yes   No*

I went to Confession today.   *Yes   No*

Days since my last Confession: _____ days.

I prayed my evening prayers tonight.   *Yes   No*

Day _____ Date _____

Feast or Holiday _____

**I prayed my
morning prayers today.**

Yes *No*

Use the Prayer Prompts to help you pray quietly. Then journal on the lines below.

_____

_____

_____

_____

_____

_____

_____

_____

_____

_____

_____

_____

_____

_____

_____

_____

_____

I went to Mass today.   *Yes*   *No*

I prayed _____ decades of the Holy Rosary today.

I examined my conscience today.   *Yes*   *No*

I went to Confession today.   *Yes*   *No*

Days since my last Confession: _____ days.

I prayed my evening prayers tonight.   *Yes*   *No*

Day _____ Date _____

Feast or Holiday _____

I prayed my
morning prayers today.

Yes   *No*

Use the Prayer Prompts to help you pray quietly. Then journal on the lines below.

....

....

....

....

....

....

....

....

....

....

....

....

....

....

....

I went to Mass today.   *Yes   No*

I prayed _____ decades of the Holy Rosary today.

I examined my conscience today.   *Yes   No*

I went to Confession today.   *Yes   No*

Days since my last Confession: _____ days.

I prayed my evening prayers tonight.   *Yes   No*

Day _____ Date _____

Feast or Holiday _____

I prayed my
morning prayers today.

Yes   *No*

Use the Prayer Prompts to help you pray quietly. Then journal on the lines below.

I went to Mass today.   *Yes   No*
I prayed _____ decades of the Holy Rosary today.
I examined my conscience today.   *Yes   No*

I went to Confession today.   *Yes   No*
Days since my last Confession: _____ days.
I prayed my evening prayers tonight.   *Yes   No*

Day _____ Date _____

Feast or Holiday _____

**I prayed my
morning prayers today.**

Yes   No

Use the Prayer Prompts to help you pray quietly. Then journal on the lines below.

_____

_____

_____

_____

_____

_____

_____

_____

_____

_____

_____

_____

went to Mass today. *Yes No*	I went to Confession today. *Yes No*
prayed _____ decades of the Holy Rosary today.	Days since my last Confession: _____ days.
examined my conscience today. *Yes No*	I prayed my evening prayers tonight. *Yes No*

Day _____   Date _____

Feast or Holiday _____

I prayed my
morning prayers today.

Yes   *No*

Use the Prayer Prompts to help you pray quietly. Then journal on the lines below.

_____

_____

_____

_____

_____

_____

_____

_____

_____

_____

_____

_____

_____

_____

_____

_____

I went to Mass today.   *Yes*   *No*

I prayed _____ decades of the Holy Rosary today.

I examined my conscience today.   *Yes*   *No*

I went to Confession today.   *Yes*   *No*

Days since my last Confession: _____ days.

I prayed my evening prayers tonight.   *Yes*   *No*

Day _____ Date _____

Feast or Holiday _____

I prayed my
morning prayers today.

Yes   *No*

Use the Prayer Prompts to help you pray quietly. Then journal on the lines below.

....

....

....

....

....

....

....

....

....

....

....

....

....

....

I went to Mass today.   *Yes*   *No*

I prayed _____ decades of the Holy Rosary today.

I examined my conscience today.   *Yes*   *No*

I went to Confession today.   *Yes*   *No*

Days since my last Confession: _____ days.

I prayed my evening prayers tonight.   *Yes*   *No*

Day _____ Date _____

Feast or Holiday _____

I prayed my morning prayers today.

Yes   No

Use the Prayer Prompts to help you pray quietly. Then journal on the lines below.

_____

_____

_____

_____

_____

_____

_____

_____

_____

_____

_____

_____

_____

_____

_____

I went to Mass today.   *Yes   No*

I prayed _____ decades of the Holy Rosary today.

I examined my conscience today.   *Yes   No*

I went to Confession today.   *Yes   No*

Days since my last Confession: _____ days.

I prayed my evening prayers tonight.   *Yes   No*

Day _____ Date _____

Feast or Holiday _____

I prayed my
morning prayers today.

Yes   *No*

Use the Prayer Prompts to help you pray quietly. Then journal on the lines below.

I went to Mass today.   *Yes*   *No*

I prayed _____ decades of the Holy Rosary today.

I examined my conscience today.   *Yes*   *No*

I went to Confession today.   *Yes*   *No*

Days since my last Confession: _____ days.

I prayed my evening prayers tonight.   *Yes*   *No*

Day _____ Date _____

Feast or Holiday _____

**I prayed my
morning prayers today.**

Yes   *No*

Use the Prayer Prompts to help you pray quietly. Then journal on the lines below.

....

....

....

....

....

....

....

....

....

....

....

....

....

....

....

I went to Mass today.   *Yes*   *No*

I prayed _____ decades of the Holy Rosary today.

I examined my conscience today.   *Yes*   *No*

I went to Confession today.   *Yes*   *No*

Days since my last Confession: _____ days.

I prayed my evening prayers tonight.   *Yes*   *No*

Day _____ Date _____

Feast or Holiday _____

I prayed my
morning prayers today.

Yes   No

Use the Prayer Prompts to help you pray quietly. Then journal on the lines below.

....

....

....

....

....

....

....

....

....

....

....

....

....

....

I went to Mass today.   Yes   No

I prayed _____ decades of the Holy Rosary today.

I examined my conscience today.   Yes   No

I went to Confession today.   Yes   No

Days since my last Confession: _____ days.

I prayed my evening prayers tonight.   Yes   No

Day _____ Date _____

Feast or Holiday _____

I prayed my morning prayers today.

Yes   No

Use the Prayer Prompts to help you pray quietly. Then journal on the lines below.

_____

_____

_____

_____

_____

_____

_____

_____

_____

_____

_____

_____

_____

_____

_____

_____

I went to Mass today.   *Yes   No*

I prayed _____ decades of the Holy Rosary today.

I examined my conscience today.   *Yes   No*

I went to Confession today.   *Yes   No*

Days since my last Confession: _____ days.

I prayed my evening prayers tonight.   *Yes   No*

Day _____ Date _____

Feast or Holiday _____

**I prayed my
morning prayers today.**

Yes   *No*

Use the Prayer Prompts to help you pray quietly. Then journal on the lines below.

....

....

....

....

....

....

....

....

....

....

....

....

....

....

I went to Mass today.   *Yes*   *No*

I prayed _____ decades of the Holy Rosary today.

I examined my conscience today.   *Yes*   *No*

I went to Confession today.   *Yes*   *No*

Days since my last Confession: _____ days.

I prayed my evening prayers tonight.   *Yes*   *No*

Day	Date	I prayed my
		morning prayers today.
Feast or Holiday		Yes No

Use the Prayer Prompts to help you pray quietly. Then journal on the lines below.

....

....

....

....

....

....

....

....

....

....

....

....

....

....

I went to Mass today.   *Yes   No*

I prayed _____ decades of the Holy Rosary today.

I examined my conscience today.   *Yes   No*

I went to Confession today.   *Yes   No*

Days since my last Confession: _____ days.

I prayed my evening prayers tonight.   *Yes   No*

Day _____ Date _____

Feast or Holiday _____

I prayed my
morning prayers today.

Yes   No

Use the Prayer Prompts to help you pray quietly. Then journal on the lines below.

....

....

....

....

....

....

....

....

....

....

....

....

....

....

....

....

....

I went to Mass today.   *Yes   No*

I prayed _____ decades of the Holy Rosary today.

I examined my conscience today.   *Yes   No*

I went to Confession today.   *Yes   No*

Days since my last Confession: _____ days.

I prayed my evening prayers tonight.   *Yes   No*

Day _____ Date _____

Feast or Holiday _____

I prayed my morning prayers today.

Yes   No

Use the Prayer Prompts to help you pray quietly. Then journal on the lines below.

....

....

....

....

....

....

....

....

....

....

....

....

....

....

I went to Mass today.   *Yes   No*

I prayed _____ decades of the Holy Rosary today.

I examined my conscience today.   *Yes   No*

I went to Confession today.   *Yes   No*

Days since my last Confession: _____ days.

I prayed my evening prayers tonight.   *Yes   No*

Day _____ Date _____

Feast or Holiday _____

I prayed my
morning prayers today.

Yes   *No*

Use the Prayer Prompts to help you pray quietly. Then journal on the lines below.

I went to Mass today.   *Yes*   *No*

I prayed _____ decades of the Holy Rosary today.

I examined my conscience today.   *Yes*   *No*

I went to Confession today.   *Yes*   *No*

Days since my last Confession: _____ days.

I prayed my evening prayers tonight.   *Yes*   *No*

Day _____ Date _____

Feast or Holiday _____

I prayed my
morning prayers today.

Yes   *No*

Use the Prayer Prompts to help you pray quietly. Then journal on the lines below.

_____

_____

_____

_____

_____

_____

_____

_____

_____

_____

_____

_____

_____

_____

_____

I went to Mass today.   *Yes*   *No*

I prayed _____ decades of the Holy Rosary today.

I examined my conscience today.   *Yes*   *No*

I went to Confession today.   *Yes*   *No*

Days since my last Confession: _____ days.

I prayed my evening prayers tonight.   *Yes*   *No*

Day _____ Date _____

Feast or Holiday _____

I prayed my
morning prayers today.

Yes   *No*

Use the Prayer Prompts to help you pray quietly. Then journal on the lines below.

....

....

....

....

....

....

....

....

....

....

....

....

....

....

....

I went to Mass today.   *Yes*   *No*

I prayed _____ decades of the Holy Rosary today.

I examined my conscience today.   *Yes*   *No*

I went to Confession today.   *Yes*   *No*

Days since my last Confession: _____ days.

I prayed my evening prayers tonight.   *Yes*   *No*

Day _____ Date _____

Feast or Holiday _____

I prayed my
morning prayers today.

Yes   *No*

Use the Prayer Prompts to help you pray quietly. Then journal on the lines below.

I went to Mass today.   *Yes*   *No*

I prayed _____ decades of the Holy Rosary today.

I examined my conscience today.   *Yes*   *No*

I went to Confession today.   *Yes*   *No*

Days since my last Confession: _____ days.

I prayed my evening prayers tonight.   *Yes*   *No*

Day _____ Date _____

Feast or Holiday _____

I prayed my
morning prayers today.

Yes   No

Use the Prayer Prompts to help you pray quietly. Then journal on the lines below.

_____

_____

_____

_____

_____

_____

_____

_____

_____

_____

_____

_____

_____

_____

_____

_____

I went to Mass today.   *Yes   No*

I prayed _____ decades of the Holy Rosary today.

I examined my conscience today.   *Yes   No*

I went to Confession today.   *Yes   No*

Days since my last Confession: _____ days.

I prayed my evening prayers tonight.   *Yes   No*

Day _____   Date _____

Feast or Holiday _____

I prayed my
morning prayers today.

Yes   *No*

Use the Prayer Prompts to help you pray quietly. Then journal on the lines below.

....

....

....

....

....

....

....

....

....

....

....

....

....

....

....

....

I went to Mass today.   *Yes*   *No*

I prayed _____ decades of the Holy Rosary today.

I examined my conscience today.   *Yes*   *No*

I went to Confession today.   *Yes*   *No*

Days since my last Confession: _____ days.

I prayed my evening prayers tonight.   *Yes*   *No*

Day _____ Date _____

Feast or Holiday _____

I prayed my
morning prayers today.

Yes   No

Use the Prayer Prompts to help you pray quietly. Then journal on the lines below.

....

....

....

....

....

....

....

....

....

....

....

....

....

....

....

....

I went to Mass today.   *Yes   No*

I prayed _____ decades of the Holy Rosary today.

I examined my conscience today.   *Yes   No*

I went to Confession today.   *Yes   No*

Days since my last Confession: _____ days.

I prayed my evening prayers tonight.   *Yes   No*

Day _____ Date _____

Feast or Holiday _____

I prayed my
morning prayers today.

Yes   No

Use the Prayer Prompts to help you pray quietly. Then journal on the lines below.

_____

_____

_____

_____

_____

_____

_____

_____

_____

_____

_____

_____

_____

_____

_____

_____

_____

I went to Mass today.   Yes   No

I prayed _____ decades of the Holy Rosary today.

I examined my conscience today.   Yes   No

I went to Confession today.   Yes   No

Days since my last Confession: _____ days.

I prayed my evening prayers tonight.   Yes   No

Day _____ Date _____

I prayed my
morning prayers today.

Feast or Holiday _____

Yes   *No*

Use the Prayer Prompts to help you pray quietly. Then journal on the lines below.

....

....

....

....

....

....

....

....

....

....

....

....

....

....

....

....

....

I went to Mass today.   *Yes   No*

I went to Confession today.   *Yes   No*

I prayed _____ decades of the Holy Rosary today.

Days since my last Confession: _____ days.

I examined my conscience today.   *Yes   No*

I prayed my evening prayers tonight.   *Yes   No*

Use the Prayer Prompts to help you pray quietly. Then journal on the lines below.

....

....

....

....

....

....

....

....

....

....

....

....

....

....

....

I went to Mass today.   *Yes*   *No*

I prayed _____ decades of the Holy Rosary today.

I examined my conscience today.   *Yes*   *No*

I went to Confession today.   *Yes*   *No*

Days since my last Confession: _____ days.

I prayed my evening prayers tonight.   *Yes*   *No*

Day _____ Date _____

Feast or Holiday _____

I prayed my
morning prayers today.

Yes   *No*

Use the Prayer Prompts to help you pray quietly. Then journal on the lines below.

_____

_____

_____

_____

_____

_____

_____

_____

_____

_____

_____

_____

_____

_____

_____

_____

I went to Mass today.   *Yes*   *No*

I prayed _____ decades of the Holy Rosary today.

I examined my conscience today.   *Yes*   *No*

I went to Confession today.   *Yes*   *No*

Days since my last Confession: _____ days.

I prayed my evening prayers tonight.   *Yes*   *No*

Day _____ Date _____

Feast or Holiday _____

I prayed my morning prayers today.

Yes   No

Use the Prayer Prompts to help you pray quietly. Then journal on the lines below.

....

....

....

....

....

....

....

....

....

....

....

....

....

....

_____

I went to Mass today.   *Yes   No*

I prayed _____ decades of the Holy Rosary today.

I examined my conscience today.   *Yes   No*

I went to Confession today.   *Yes   No*

Days since my last Confession: _____ days.

I prayed my evening prayers tonight.   *Yes   No*

Day _____ Date _____

Feast or Holiday _____

I prayed my
morning prayers today.

Yes   *No*

Use the Prayer Prompts to help you pray quietly. Then journal on the lines below.

I went to Mass today.   *Yes*   *No*

I prayed _____ decades of the Holy Rosary today.

I examined my conscience today.   *Yes*   *No*

I went to Confession today.   *Yes*   *No*

Days since my last Confession: _____ days.

I prayed my evening prayers tonight.   *Yes*   *No*

Day _____ Date _____

Feast or Holiday _____

I prayed my morning prayers today.

Yes   No

Use the Prayer Prompts to help you pray quietly. Then journal on the lines below.

_____
_____
_____
_____
_____
_____
_____
_____
_____
_____
_____
_____
_____

I went to Mass today.   *Yes   No*

I prayed _____ decades of the Holy Rosary today.

I examined my conscience today.   *Yes   No*

I went to Confession today.   *Yes   No*

Days since my last Confession: _____ days.

I prayed my evening prayers tonight.   *Yes   No*

Day _____ Date _____

Feast or Holiday _____

I prayed my
morning prayers today.

Yes   No

Use the Prayer Prompts to help you pray quietly. Then journal on the lines below.

....

....

....

....

....

....

....

....

....

....

....

....

....

....

....

....

....

....

....

I went to Mass today.   Yes   No

I prayed _____ decades of the Holy Rosary today.

I examined my conscience today.   Yes   No

I went to Confession today.   Yes   No

Days since my last Confession: _____ days.

I prayed my evening prayers tonight.   Yes   No

Day _____ Date _____

Feast or Holiday _____

**I prayed my
morning prayers today.**

Yes   No

Use the Prayer Prompts to help you pray quietly. Then journal on the lines below.

....

....

....

....

....

....

....

....

....

....

....

....

....

....

....

....

I went to Mass today.   *Yes   No*

I prayed _____ decades of the Holy Rosary today.

I examined my conscience today.   *Yes   No*

I went to Confession today.   *Yes   No*

Days since my last Confession: _____ days.

I prayed my evening prayers tonight.   *Yes   No*

Day _____ Date _____

Feast or Holiday _____

I prayed my
morning prayers today.

Yes   *No*

Use the Prayer Prompts to help you pray quietly. Then journal on the lines below.

....

....

....

....

....

....

....

....

....

....

....

....

....

....

....

....

I went to Mass today.   *Yes   No*

I prayed _____ decades of the Holy Rosary today.

I examined my conscience today.   *Yes   No*

I went to Confession today.   *Yes   No*

Days since my last Confession: _____ days.

I prayed my evening prayers tonight.   *Yes   No*

Day _____ Date _____

Feast or Holiday _____

I prayed my
morning prayers today.

Yes   *No*

Use the Prayer Prompts to help you pray quietly. Then journal on the lines below.

I went to Mass today.   *Yes*   *No*

I prayed _____ decades of the Holy Rosary today.

I examined my conscience today.   *Yes*   *No*

I went to Confession today.   *Yes*   *No*

Days since my last Confession: _____ days.

I prayed my evening prayers tonight.   *Yes*   *No*

Day _____ Date _____

Feast or Holiday _____

I prayed my
morning prayers today.

Yes   No

Use the Prayer Prompts to help you pray quietly. Then journal on the lines below.

_____

_____

_____

_____

_____

_____

_____

_____

_____

_____

_____

_____

_____

_____

I went to Mass today.   *Yes   No*

I prayed _____ decades of the Holy Rosary today.

I examined my conscience today.   *Yes   No*

I went to Confession today.   *Yes   No*

Days since my last Confession: _____ days.

I prayed my evening prayers tonight.   *Yes   No*

Day _____ Date _____

Feast or Holiday _____

**I prayed my
morning prayers today.**

Yes   No

Use the Prayer Prompts to help you pray quietly. Then journal on the lines below.

....

....

....

....

....

....

....

....

....

....

....

....

....

....

I went to Mass today.   *Yes   No*

I prayed _____ decades of the Holy Rosary today.

I examined my conscience today.   *Yes   No*

I went to Confession today.   *Yes   No*

Days since my last Confession: _____ days.

I prayed my evening prayers tonight.   *Yes   No*

Day _____ Date _____

Feast or Holiday _____

I prayed my
morning prayers today.

Yes   No

Use the Prayer Prompts to help you pray quietly. Then journal on the lines below.

....

....

....

....

....

....

....

....

....

....

....

....

....

I went to Mass today.   Yes   No

I prayed _____ decades of the Holy Rosary today.

I examined my conscience today.   Yes   No

I went to Confession today.   Yes   No

Days since my last Confession: _____ days.

I prayed my evening prayers tonight.   Yes   No

Day _____ Date _____

Feast or Holiday _____

I prayed my
morning prayers today.

Yes   *No*

Use the Prayer Prompts to help you pray quietly. Then journal on the lines below.

I went to Mass today.   *Yes*   *No*

I prayed _____ decades of the Holy Rosary today.

I examined my conscience today.   *Yes*   *No*

I went to Confession today.   *Yes*   *No*

Days since my last Confession: _____ days.

I prayed my evening prayers tonight.   *Yes*   *No*

Day _____ Date _____

Feast or Holiday _____

I prayed my
morning prayers today.

Yes   No

Use the Prayer Prompts to help you pray quietly. Then journal on the lines below.

_____

_____

_____

_____

_____

_____

_____

_____

_____

_____

_____

_____

_____

_____

_____

_____

I went to Mass today.   *Yes   No*

I prayed _____ decades of the Holy Rosary today.

I examined my conscience today.   *Yes   No*

I went to Confession today.   *Yes   No*

Days since my last Confession: _____ days.

I prayed my evening prayers tonight.   *Yes   No*

Day _____ Date _____

Feast or Holiday _____

I prayed my
morning prayers today.

Yes   *No*

Use the Prayer Prompts to help you pray quietly. Then journal on the lines below.

I went to Mass today.   *Yes*   *No*

I prayed _____ decades of the Holy Rosary today.

I examined my conscience today.   *Yes*   *No*

I went to Confession today.   *Yes*   *No*

Days since my last Confession: _____ days.

I prayed my evening prayers tonight.   *Yes*   *No*

Day _____   Date _____

I prayed my
morning prayers today.

Feast or Holiday _____

Yes   No

Use the Prayer Prompts to help you pray quietly. Then journal on the lines below.

....

....

....

....

....

....

....

....

....

....

....

....

....

....

....

....

I went to Mass today.   Yes   No

I prayed _____ decades of the Holy Rosary today.

I examined my conscience today.   Yes   No

I went to Confession today.   Yes   No

Days since my last Confession: _____ days.

I prayed my evening prayers tonight.   Yes   No

Day _____ Date _____

I prayed my
morning prayers today.

Yes   *No*

Feast or Holiday _____

Use the Prayer Prompts to help you pray quietly. Then journal on the lines below.

_____

_____

_____

_____

_____

_____

_____

_____

_____

_____

_____

_____

_____

_____

_____

_____

_____

_____

I went to Mass today.   *Yes   No*

I prayed _____ decades of the Holy Rosary today.

I examined my conscience today.   *Yes   No*

I went to Confession today.   *Yes   No*

Days since my last Confession: _____ days.

I prayed my evening prayers tonight.   *Yes   No*

Use the Prayer Prompts to help you pray quietly. Then journal on the lines below.

....

....

....

....

....

....

....

....

....

....

....

....

....

....

....

....

I went to Mass today.   *Yes*   *No*

I prayed _____ decades of the Holy Rosary today.

I examined my conscience today.   *Yes*   *No*

I went to Confession today.   *Yes*   *No*

Days since my last Confession: _____ days.

I prayed my evening prayers tonight.   *Yes*   *No*

Day _____ Date _____

Feast or Holiday _____

I prayed my
morning prayers today.

Yes   *No*

Use the Prayer Prompts to help you pray quietly. Then journal on the lines below.

_____

_____

_____

_____

_____

_____

_____

_____

_____

_____

_____

_____

_____

_____

_____

I went to Mass today.   *Yes   No*

I prayed _____ decades of the Holy Rosary today.

I examined my conscience today.   *Yes   No*

I went to Confession today.   *Yes   No*

Days since my last Confession: _____ days.

I prayed my evening prayers tonight.   *Yes   No*

Day _____ Date _____

Feast or Holiday _____

**I prayed my
morning prayers today.**

Yes   *No*

Use the Prayer Prompts to help you pray quietly. Then journal on the lines below.

_____

_____

_____

_____

_____

_____

_____

_____

_____

_____

_____

_____

_____

_____

_____

_____

_____

I went to Mass today.   *Yes   No*

I prayed _____ decades of the Holy Rosary today.

I examined my conscience today.   *Yes   No*

I went to Confession today.   *Yes   No*

Days since my last Confession: _____ days.

I prayed my evening prayers tonight.   *Yes   No*

Day _____ Date _____

Feast or Holiday _____

**I prayed my
morning prayers today.**

Yes   No

Use the Prayer Prompts to help you pray quietly. Then journal on the lines below.

_____

_____

_____

_____

_____

_____

_____

_____

_____

_____

_____

_____

_____

_____

I went to Mass today.   *Yes   No*

I prayed _____ decades of the Holy Rosary today.

I examined my conscience today.   *Yes   No*

I went to Confession today.   *Yes   No*

Days since my last Confession: _____ days.

I prayed my evening prayers tonight.   *Yes   No*

Day _____ Date _____

Feast or Holiday _____

I prayed my
morning prayers today.

Yes   *No*

Use the Prayer Prompts to help you pray quietly. Then journal on the lines below.

....

....

....

....

....

....

....

....

....

....

....

....

....

....

I went to Mass today.   *Yes*   *No*

I prayed _____ decades of the Holy Rosary today.

I examined my conscience today.   *Yes*   *No*

I went to Confession today.   *Yes*   *No*

Days since my last Confession: _____ days.

I prayed my evening prayers tonight.   *Yes*   *No*

Day _____ Date _____

Feast or Holiday _____

I prayed my
morning prayers today.

Yes   No

Use the Prayer Prompts to help you pray quietly. Then journal on the lines below.

....

....

....

....

....

....

....

....

....

....

....

....

....

....

....

I went to Mass today.   *Yes   No*

I prayed _____ decades of the Holy Rosary today.

I examined my conscience today.   *Yes   No*

I went to Confession today.   *Yes   No*

Days since my last Confession: _____ days.

I prayed my evening prayers tonight.   *Yes   No*

Day _____ Date _____

Feast or Holiday _____

I prayed my
morning prayers today.

Yes   *No*

Use the Prayer Prompts to help you pray quietly. Then journal on the lines below.

....

....

....

....

....

....

....

....

....

....

....

....

....

....

I went to Mass today.   *Yes*   *No*

I prayed _____ decades of the Holy Rosary today.

I examined my conscience today.   *Yes*   *No*

I went to Confession today.   *Yes*   *No*

Days since my last Confession: _____ days.

I prayed my evening prayers tonight.   *Yes*   *No*

Day _____ Date _____

Feast or Holiday _____

I prayed my morning prayers today.

Yes   *No*

Use the Prayer Prompts to help you pray quietly. Then journal on the lines below.

_____

_____

_____

_____

_____

_____

_____

_____

_____

_____

_____

_____

_____

_____

I went to Mass today.   *Yes*   *No*

I prayed _____ decades of the Holy Rosary today.

I examined my conscience today.   *Yes*   *No*

I went to Confession today.   *Yes*   *No*

Days since my last Confession: _____ days.

I prayed my evening prayers tonight.   *Yes*   *No*

Day _____ Date _____

Feast or Holiday _____

I prayed my
morning prayers today.

Yes   *No*

Use the Prayer Prompts to help you pray quietly. Then journal on the lines below.

....

....

....

....

....

....

....

....

....

....

....

....

....

....

....

....

I went to Mass today.   *Yes*   *No*

I prayed _____ decades of the Holy Rosary today.

I examined my conscience today.   *Yes*   *No*

I went to Confession today.   *Yes*   *No*

Days since my last Confession: _____ days.

I prayed my evening prayers tonight.   *Yes*   *No*

Use the Prayer Prompts to help you pray quietly. Then journal on the lines below.

_____

_____

_____

_____

_____

_____

_____

_____

_____

_____

_____

_____

_____

I went to Mass today.   *Yes*   *No*

I prayed _____ decades of the Holy Rosary today.

I examined my conscience today.   *Yes*   *No*

I went to Confession today.   *Yes*   *No*

Days since my last Confession: _____ days.

I prayed my evening prayers tonight.   *Yes*   *No*

Day _____ Date _____

Feast or Holiday _____

I prayed my
morning prayers today.

Yes   *No*

Use the Prayer Prompts to help you pray quietly. Then journal on the lines below.

I went to Mass today.   *Yes*   *No*

I prayed _____ decades of the Holy Rosary today.

I examined my conscience today.   *Yes*   *No*

I went to Confession today.   *Yes*   *No*

Days since my last Confession: _____ days.

I prayed my evening prayers tonight.   *Yes*   *No*

Day _____ Date _____

Feast or Holiday _____

I prayed my
morning prayers today.

Yes   No

Use the Prayer Prompts to help you pray quietly. Then journal on the lines below.

....

....

....

....

....

....

....

....

....

....

....

....

....

....

....

....

I went to Mass today.   *Yes   No*

I prayed _____ decades of the Holy Rosary today.

I examined my conscience today.   *Yes   No*

I went to Confession today.   *Yes   No*

Days since my last Confession: _____ days.

I prayed my evening prayers tonight.   *Yes   No*

Day _____ Date _____

Feast or Holiday _____

I prayed my
morning prayers today.

Yes   *No*

Use the Prayer Prompts to help you pray quietly. Then journal on the lines below.

....

....

....

....

....

....

....

....

....

....

....

....

....

....

....

....

....

....

I went to Mass today.   *Yes*   *No*

I prayed _____ decades of the Holy Rosary today.

I examined my conscience today.   *Yes*   *No*

I went to Confession today.   *Yes*   *No*

Days since my last Confession: _____ days.

I prayed my evening prayers tonight.   *Yes*   *No*

Day _____ Date _____

Feast or Holiday _____

I prayed my
morning prayers today.

Yes   *No*

Use the Prayer Prompts to help you pray quietly. Then journal on the lines below.

....

....

....

....

....

....

....

....

....

....

....

....

....

....

I went to Mass today.   *Yes*   *No*

I prayed _____ decades of the Holy Rosary today.

I examined my conscience today.   *Yes*   *No*

I went to Confession today.   *Yes*   *No*

Days since my last Confession: _____ days.

I prayed my evening prayers tonight.   *Yes*   *No*

Day _____ Date _____

Feast or Holiday _____

I prayed my
morning prayers today.

Yes   *No*

Use the Prayer Prompts to help you pray quietly. Then journal on the lines below.

....

....

....

....

....

....

....

....

....

....

....

....

....

....

....

....

....

I went to Mass today.   *Yes*   *No*

I prayed _____ decades of the Holy Rosary today.

I examined my conscience today.   *Yes*   *No*

I went to Confession today.   *Yes*   *No*

Days since my last Confession: _____ days.

I prayed my evening prayers tonight.   *Yes*   *No*

Day _____ Date _____

Feast or Holiday _____

I prayed my
morning prayers today.

Yes   *No*

Use the Prayer Prompts to help you pray quietly. Then journal on the lines below.

I went to Mass today.   *Yes*   *No*

I prayed _____ decades of the Holy Rosary today.

I examined my conscience today.   *Yes*   *No*

I went to Confession today.   *Yes*   *No*

Days since my last Confession: _____ days.

I prayed my evening prayers tonight.   *Yes*   *No*

Day _____ Date _____

Feast or Holiday _____

I prayed my
morning prayers today.

Yes   No

Use the Prayer Prompts to help you pray quietly. Then journal on the lines below.

I went to Mass today.   Yes   No

I prayed _____ decades of the Holy Rosary today.

I examined my conscience today.   Yes   No

I went to Confession today.   Yes   No

Days since my last Confession: _____ days.

I prayed my evening prayers tonight.   Yes   No

Day _____ Date _____

Feast or Holiday _____

I prayed my
morning prayers today.

Yes   No

Use the Prayer Prompts to help you pray quietly. Then journal on the lines below.

....

....

....

....

....

....

....

....

....

....

....

....

....

....

....

I went to Mass today.   Yes   No

I prayed _____ decades of the Holy Rosary today.

I examined my conscience today.   Yes   No

I went to Confession today.   Yes   No

Days since my last Confession: _____ days.

I prayed my evening prayers tonight.   Yes   No

Day _____ Date _____

Feast or Holiday _____

**I prayed my
morning prayers today.**

Yes   No

Use the Prayer Prompts to help you pray quietly. Then journal on the lines below.

....

....

....

....

....

....

....

....

....

....

....

....

....

....

I went to Mass today.   *Yes   No*

I prayed _____ decades of the Holy Rosary today.

I examined my conscience today.   *Yes   No*

I went to Confession today.   *Yes   No*

Days since my last Confession: _____ days.

I prayed my evening prayers tonight.   *Yes   No*

Day _____ Date _____

Feast or Holiday _____

I prayed my morning prayers today.

Yes   No

Use the Prayer Prompts to help you pray quietly. Then journal on the lines below.

_____

_____

_____

_____

_____

_____

_____

_____

_____

_____

_____

_____

_____

_____

_____

I went to Mass today.   *Yes   No*

I prayed _____ decades of the Holy Rosary today.

I examined my conscience today.   *Yes   No*

I went to Confession today.   *Yes   No*

Days since my last Confession: _____ days.

I prayed my evening prayers tonight.   *Yes   No*

Day _____ Date _____

Feast or Holiday _____

I prayed my
morning prayers today.

Yes   *No*

Use the Prayer Prompts to help you pray quietly. Then journal on the lines below.

....

....

....

....

....

....

....

....

....

....

....

....

....

....

I went to Mass today.   *Yes   No*

I prayed _____ decades of the Holy Rosary today.

I examined my conscience today.   *Yes   No*

I went to Confession today.   *Yes   No*

Days since my last Confession: _____ days.

I prayed my evening prayers tonight.   *Yes   No*

Day _____ Date _____

Feast or Holiday _____

**I prayed my
morning prayers today.**

Yes   *No*

Use the Prayer Prompts to help you pray quietly. Then journal on the lines below.

I went to Mass today.   *Yes*   *No*

I prayed _____ decades of the Holy Rosary today.

I examined my conscience today.   *Yes*   *No*

I went to Confession today.   *Yes*   *No*

Days since my last Confession: _____ days.

I prayed my evening prayers tonight.   *Yes*   *No*

Day _____   Date _____

Feast or Holiday _____

I prayed my
morning prayers today.

Yes   *No*

Use the Prayer Prompts to help you pray quietly. Then journal on the lines below.

....

....

....

....

....

....

....

....

....

....

....

....

....

....

I went to Mass today.   *Yes   No*

I prayed _____ decades of the Holy Rosary today.

I examined my conscience today.   *Yes   No*

I went to Confession today.   *Yes   No*

Days since my last Confession: _____ days.

I prayed my evening prayers tonight.   *Yes   No*

Day _____ Date _____

Feast or Holiday _____

I prayed my
morning prayers today.

Yes   No

Use the Prayer Prompts to help you pray quietly. Then journal on the lines below.

_____

_____

_____

_____

_____

_____

_____

_____

_____

_____

_____

_____

_____

_____

I went to Mass today.   Yes   No

I prayed _____ decades of the Holy Rosary today.

I examined my conscience today.   Yes   No

I went to Confession today.   Yes   No

Days since my last Confession: _____ days.

I prayed my evening prayers tonight.   Yes   No

Day _____ Date _____

Feast or Holiday _____

I prayed my
morning prayers today.

Yes   No

Use the Prayer Prompts to help you pray quietly. Then journal on the lines below.

_____

_____

_____

_____

_____

_____

_____

_____

_____

_____

_____

_____

_____

_____

_____

I went to Mass today.   *Yes   No*

I prayed _____ decades of the Holy Rosary today.

I examined my conscience today.   *Yes   No*

I went to Confession today.   *Yes   No*

Days since my last Confession: _____ days.

I prayed my evening prayers tonight.   *Yes   No*

Day _____ Date _____

Feast or Holiday _____

I prayed my
morning prayers today.

Yes   *No*

Use the Prayer Prompts to help you pray quietly. Then journal on the lines below.

I went to Mass today.   *Yes*   *No*

I prayed _____ decades of the Holy Rosary today.

I examined my conscience today.   *Yes*   *No*

I went to Confession today.   *Yes*   *No*

Days since my last Confession: _____ days.

I prayed my evening prayers tonight.   *Yes*   *No*

Day _____ Date _____

Feast or Holiday _____

I prayed my
morning prayers today.

Yes   *No*

Use the Prayer Prompts to help you pray quietly. Then journal on the lines below.

....

....

....

....

....

....

....

....

....

....

....

....

....

....

went to Mass today.   *Yes   No*

prayed _____ decades of the Holy Rosary today.

examined my conscience today.   *Yes   No*

I went to Confession today.   *Yes   No*

Days since my last Confession: _____ days.

I prayed my evening prayers tonight.   *Yes   No*

Day _____ Date _____

Feast or Holiday _____

I prayed my
morning prayers today.

Yes   *No*

Use the Prayer Prompts to help you pray quietly. Then journal on the lines below.

....

....

....

....

....

....

....

....

....

....

....

....

....

....

I went to Mass today.   *Yes*   *No*

I prayed _____ decades of the Holy Rosary today.

I examined my conscience today.   *Yes*   *No*

I went to Confession today.   *Yes*   *No*

Days since my last Confession: _____ days.

I prayed my evening prayers tonight.   *Yes*   *No*

Day _____ Date _____

Feast or Holiday _____

I prayed my
morning prayers today.

Yes   *No*

Use the Prayer Prompts to help you pray quietly. Then journal on the lines below.

....

....

....

....

....

....

....

....

....

....

....

....

....

I went to Mass today.   *Yes*   *No*

I prayed _____ decades of the Holy Rosary today.

I examined my conscience today.   *Yes*   *No*

I went to Confession today.   *Yes*   *No*

Days since my last Confession: _____ days.

I prayed my evening prayers tonight.   *Yes*   *No*

Day _____ Date _____

Feast or Holiday _____

I prayed my morning prayers today.

Yes *No*

Use the Prayer Prompts to help you pray quietly. Then journal on the lines below.

....

....

....

....

....

....

....

....

....

....

....

....

....

....

....

....

I went to Mass today.   *Yes   No*

I prayed _____ decades of the Holy Rosary today.

I examined my conscience today.   *Yes   No*

I went to Confession today.   *Yes   No*

Days since my last Confession: _____ days.

I prayed my evening prayers tonight.   *Yes   No*

Day _____ Date _____

Feast or Holiday _____

I prayed my
morning prayers today.

Yes   *No*

Use the Prayer Prompts to help you pray quietly. Then journal on the lines below.

_____

_____

_____

_____

_____

_____

_____

_____

_____

_____

_____

_____

_____

_____

I went to Mass today.   *Yes*   *No*

I prayed _____ decades of the Holy Rosary today.

I examined my conscience today.   *Yes*   *No*

I went to Confession today.   *Yes*   *No*

Days since my last Confession: _____ days.

I prayed my evening prayers tonight.   *Yes*   *No*

Examination of Conscience for Confession

Ask the Holy Spirit to help you remember and recognize how you have sinned:

"Come, Holy Spirit, enlighten my mind to clearly see the sins of my life, then strengthen me to confess them honestly and completely so I can enjoy the peace of forgiveness."

Use the below to help examine your conscience since your last Confession:

Sins against the Ten Commandments

1. Did I always put God before anyone or anything else in my life?
2. Did I always think and speak reverently about God, His saints, and sacred things?
3. Did I keep the Lord's Day holy in all that I did?
4. Did I honor and respect my parents?
5. Did I harm people in any way, even in my thoughts or words?
6. Did I do anything impure or immodest with my body?
7. Did I steal, cheat, not share, or waste?
8. Did I lie, gossip, or betray someone's trust, or was I dishonest in any way?
9. Did I think about, look at, or listen to impure or immodest things?
10. Did I envy other people's success or want their things?

Sins of Omission and Waste (things I could have done, but did not)

1. Did I not forgive?
2. Did I not love other people as much as I could have?
3. Did I not show mercy to others?
4. Did I waste my time, talents, or graces from God?
5. Did I not offer my suffering and penances to God for the salvation of souls?

Tear-Out Sheet for Confession

Write your sins on the lines below as you examine your conscience. Tear the sheet out and take it with you to Confession ... it will help you to remember all the steps to make a good Confession.

Step 1 Examine your conscience and write your sins on the lines below (and on the back of this sheet), so you remember them. Include how many times you did each sin.

Step 2 Enter the confessional—kneel at the screen or sit to confess face-to-face with the priest.

Step 3 Make the Sign of the Cross, saying, **"In the Name of the Father, and of the Son, and of the Holy Spirit."**

Step 4 Say to the priest, **"Bless me, Father, for I have sinned. It has been** _____ (say how long) **since my last Confession, and these are my sins."**

(Turn this sheet over for more lines and for the rest of the steps to making a good Confession)

_____

_____

_____

_____

_____

_____

_____

_____

_____

_____

_____

More lines to write sins on:

_____

_____

_____

_____

_____

_____

_____

_____

Step 5 Confess all the sins you remember, then say, **"For these and for all my sins, I am truly sorry."**

Step 6 Listen to what the priest tells you. Ask any questions you may have.

Step 7 The priest will tell you your penance—listen carefully, and if you don't understand, ask him to repeat or explain what he said.

Step 8 When the priest tells you to, pray the Act of Contrition:
"O my God, I am heartily sorry for having offended Thee, and I detest all my sins because I fear the loss of Heaven and the pains of Hell; but, most of all, because I have offended Thee, my God, Who art all good and worthy of all my love. I firmly resolve, with the help of Thy grace, to confess my sins, to do penance, and to amend my life. Amen."

Step 9 Listen to the priest say the words of Absolution and make the Sign of the Cross when you hear him say, "In the Name of the Father, and of the Son, and of the Holy Spirit."

Step 10 The priest will dismiss you. If he says, "Give thanks to the Lord, for He is good," you answer, **"For His mercy endures forever."** Don't forget to say, **"Thanks be to God, and to you, Father!"** before you go.

Step 11 Do your penance as soon as you can. You can also destroy this paper—these sins and any others you might have forgotten are forgiven!

Cut out this page along this line.

Tear-Out Sheet for Confession

Write your sins on the lines below as you examine your conscience. Tear the sheet out and take it with you to Confession ... it will help you to remember all the steps to make a good Confession.

Step 1 Examine your conscience and write your sins on the lines below (and on the back of this sheet), so you remember them. Include how many times you did each sin.

Step 2 Enter the confessional—kneel at the screen or sit to confess face-to-face with the priest.

Step 3 Make the Sign of the Cross, saying, **"In the Name of the Father, and of the Son, and of the Holy Spirit."**

Step 4 Say to the priest, **"Bless me, Father, for I have sinned. It has been** _____ (say how long) **since my last Confession, and these are my sins."**

(Turn this sheet over for more lines and for the rest of the steps to making a good Confession)

_____

_____

_____

_____

_____

_____

_____

_____

_____

_____

_____

More lines to write sins on:

_____

_____

_____

_____

_____

_____

_____

_____

Step 5 Confess all the sins you remember, then say, **"For these and for all my sins, I am truly sorry."**

Step 6 Listen to what the priest tells you. Ask any questions you may have.

Step 7 The priest will tell you your penance—listen carefully, and if you don't understand, ask him to repeat or explain what he said.

Step 8 When the priest tells you to, pray the Act of Contrition:
"O my God, I am heartily sorry for having offended Thee, and I detest all my sins because I fear the loss of Heaven and the pains of Hell; but, most of all, because I have offended Thee, my God, Who art all good and worthy of all my love. I firmly resolve, with the help of Thy grace, to confess my sins, to do penance, and to amend my life. Amen."

Step 9 Listen to the priest say the words of Absolution and make the Sign of the Cross when you hear him say, "In the Name of the Father, and of the Son, and of the Holy Spirit."

Step 10 The priest will dismiss you. If he says, "Give thanks to the Lord, for He is good," you answer, **"For His mercy endures forever."** Don't forget to say, **"Thanks be to God, and to you, Father!"** before you go.

Step 11 Do your penance as soon as you can. You can also destroy this paper—these sins and any others you might have forgotten are forgiven!

Tear-Out Sheet for Confession

Write your sins on the lines below as you examine your conscience. Tear the sheet out and take it with you to Confession ... it will help you to remember all the steps to make a good Confession.

Step 1 Examine your conscience and write your sins on the lines below (and on the back of this sheet), so you remember them. Include how many times you did each sin.

Step 2 Enter the confessional—kneel at the screen or sit to confess face-to-face with the priest.

Step 3 Make the Sign of the Cross, saying, **"In the Name of the Father, and of the Son, and of the Holy Spirit."**

Step 4 Say to the priest, **"Bless me, Father, for I have sinned. It has been** _____ (say how long) **since my last Confession, and these are my sins."**

(Turn this sheet over for more lines and for the rest of the steps to making a good Confession)

More lines to write sins on:

_____

_____

_____

_____

_____

_____

_____

_____

Cut out this page along this line

Step 5 Confess all the sins you remember, then say, **"For these and for all my sins, I am truly sorry."**

Step 6 Listen to what the priest tells you. Ask any questions you may have.

Step 7 The priest will tell you your penance—listen carefully, and if you don't understand, ask him to repeat or explain what he said.

Step 8 When the priest tells you to, pray the Act of Contrition:
"O my God, I am heartily sorry for having offended Thee, and I detest all my sins because I fear the loss of Heaven and the pains of Hell; but, most of all, because I have offended Thee, my God, Who art all good and worthy of all my love. I firmly resolve, with the help of Thy grace, to confess my sins, to do penance, and to amend my life. Amen."

Step 9 Listen to the priest say the words of Absolution and make the Sign of the Cross when you hear him say, "In the Name of the Father, and of the Son, and of the Holy Spirit."

Step 10 The priest will dismiss you. If he says, "Give thanks to the Lord, for He is good," you answer, **"For His mercy endures forever."** Don't forget to say, **"Thanks be to God, and to you, Father!"** before you go.

Step 11 Do your penance as soon as you can. You can also destroy this paper—these sins and any others you might have forgotten are forgiven!

Tear-Out Sheet for Confession

Write your sins on the lines below as you examine your conscience. Tear the sheet out and take it with you to Confession ... it will help you to remember all the steps to make a good Confession.

Step 1 Examine your conscience and write your sins on the lines below (and on the back of this sheet), so you remember them. Include how many times you did each sin.

Step 2 Enter the confessional—kneel at the screen or sit to confess face-to-face with the priest.

Step 3 Make the Sign of the Cross, saying, **"In the Name of the Father, and of the Son, and of the Holy Spirit."**

Step 4 Say to the priest, **"Bless me, Father, for I have sinned. It has been** _____ (say how long) **since my last Confession, and these are my sins."**

(Turn this sheet over for more lines and for the rest of the steps to making a good Confession)

_____

_____

_____

_____

_____

_____

_____

_____

_____

_____

_____

_____

More lines to write sins on:

_____

_____

_____

_____

_____

_____

_____

_____

Cut out this page along this line

Step 5 Confess all the sins you remember, then say, **"For these and for all my sins, I am truly sorry."**

Step 6 Listen to what the priest tells you. Ask any questions you may have.

Step 7 The priest will tell you your penance—listen carefully, and if you don't understand, ask him to repeat or explain what he said.

Step 8 When the priest tells you to, pray the Act of Contrition:
"O my God, I am heartily sorry for having offended Thee, and I detest all my sins because I fear the loss of Heaven and the pains of Hell; but, most of all, because I have offended Thee, my God, Who art all good and worthy of all my love. I firmly resolve, with the help of Thy grace, to confess my sins, to do penance, and to amend my life. Amen."

Step 9 Listen to the priest say the words of Absolution and make the Sign of the Cross when you hear him say, "In the Name of the Father, and of the Son, and of the Holy Spirit."

Step 10 The priest will dismiss you. If he says, "Give thanks to the Lord, for He is good," you answer, **"For His mercy endures forever."** Don't forget to say, **"Thanks be to God, and to you, Father!"** before you go.

Step 11 Do your penance as soon as you can. You can also destroy this paper—these sins and any others you might have forgotten are forgiven!

Tear-Out Sheet for Confession

Write your sins on the lines below as you examine your conscience." Tear the sheet out and take it with you to Confession ... it will help you to remember all the steps to make a good Confession.

Step 1 Examine your conscience and write your sins on the lines below (and on the back of this sheet), so you remember them. Include how many times you did each sin.

Step 2 Enter the confessional—kneel at the screen or sit to confess face-to-face with the priest.

Step 3 Make the Sign of the Cross, saying, **"In the Name of the Father, and of the Son, and of the Holy Spirit."**

Step 4 Say to the priest, **"Bless me, Father, for I have sinned. It has been** _____ (say how long) **since my last Confession, and these are my sins."**

(Turn this sheet over for more lines and for the rest of the steps to making a good Confession)

_____

_____

_____

_____

_____

_____

_____

_____

_____

_____

_____

Cut out this page along this line.

More lines to write sins on:

_____

_____

_____

_____

_____

_____

_____

_____

_____

Step 5 Confess all the sins you remember, then say, **"For these and for all my sins, I am truly sorry."**

Step 6 Listen to what the priest tells you. Ask any questions you may have.

Step 7 The priest will tell you your penance—listen carefully, and if you don't understand, ask him to repeat or explain what he said.

Step 8 When the priest tells you to, pray the Act of Contrition:
"O my God, I am heartily sorry for having offended Thee, and I detest all my sins because I fear the loss of Heaven and the pains of Hell; but, most of all, because I have offended Thee, my God, Who art all good and worthy of all my love. I firmly resolve, with the help of Thy grace, to confess my sins, to do penance, and to amend my life. Amen."

Step 9 Listen to the priest say the words of Absolution and make the Sign of the Cross when you hear him say, "In the Name of the Father, and of the Son, and of the Holy Spirit."

Step 10 The priest will dismiss you. If he says, "Give thanks to the Lord, for He is good," you answer, **"For His mercy endures forever."** Don't forget to say, **"Thanks be to God, and to you, Father!"** before you go.

Step 11 Do your penance as soon as you can. You can also destroy this paper—these sins and any others you might have forgotten are forgiven!

Tear-Out Sheet for Confession

Write your sins on the lines below as you examine your conscience. Tear the sheet out and take it with you to Confession ... it will help you to remember all the steps to make a good Confession.

Step 1   Examine your conscience and write your sins on the lines below (and on the back of this sheet), so you remember them. Include how many times you did each sin.

Step 2   Enter the confessional—kneel at the screen or sit to confess face-to-face with the priest.

Step 3   Make the Sign of the Cross, saying, **"In the Name of the Father, and of the Son, and of the Holy Spirit."**

Step 4   Say to the priest, **"Bless me, Father, for I have sinned. It has been** _____ (say how long) **since my last Confession, and these are my sins."**

(Turn this sheet over for more lines and for the rest of the steps to making a good Confession)

_____

_____

_____

_____

_____

_____

_____

_____

_____

_____

More lines to write sins on:

_____

_____

_____

_____

_____

_____

_____

_____

Step 5 Confess all the sins you remember, then say, **"For these and for all my sins, I am truly sorry."**

Step 6 Listen to what the priest tells you. Ask any questions you may have.

Step 7 The priest will tell you your penance—listen carefully, and if you don't understand, ask him to repeat or explain what he said.

Step 8 When the priest tells you to, pray the Act of Contrition:
"O my God, I am heartily sorry for having offended Thee, and I detest all my sins because I fear the loss of Heaven and the pains of Hell; but, most of all, because I have offended Thee, my God, Who art all good and worthy of all my love. I firmly resolve, with the help of Thy grace, to confess my sins, to do penance, and to amend my life. Amen."

Step 9 Listen to the priest say the words of Absolution and make the Sign of the Cross when you hear him say, "In the Name of the Father, and of the Son, and of the Holy Spirit."

Step 10 The priest will dismiss you. If he says, "Give thanks to the Lord, for He is good," you answer, **"For His mercy endures forever."** Don't forget to say, **"Thanks be to God, and to you, Father!"** before you go.

Step 11 Do your penance as soon as you can. You can also destroy this paper—these sins and any others you might have forgotten are forgiven!